CW00338421

THROUGH FIELDS OF GOLD

Tom Davies, a Welshman born and bred, trained as a journalist with the *Western Mail* and later worked for *The Sunday Times*, the *Sunday Telegraph* and *The Observer*, where for three years he was the diarist Pendennis. Now a writer, broadcaster and columnist on the *Western Mail*, he has written many books: his *Merlyn the Magician and the Pacific Coast Highway* was short-listed for the Thomas Cook Travel Book of the Year Award, while his pilgrimage narrative *Stained Glass Hours* (recently published in paperback as *Wild Skies and Celtic Paths*) won the Winifred Mary Stanford prize for the best book with a religious theme.

He lives in a coastguard tower which overlooks the Bristol Channel in Penarth, South Wales and is married with three sons.

By the same author

Novels

One Winter of the Holy Spirit (Macdonald)
Black Sunlight (Macdonald)
Fire in the Bay (Collins)
The Electric Harvest (New English Library)
I, Conker . . . (Gomer)

Travel

Merlyn the Magician and the Pacific Coast Highway (New English Library)
Stained Glass Hours (New English Library)
Landscapes of Glory (Triangle)
The Celtic Heart (Triangle)
Wild Skies and Celtic Paths (Triangle)
The Road to the Stars (Triangle)

Theology

The Man of Lawlessness (Hodder & Stoughton)
The Visions of Caradoc (Azure)

The Web

The Media, Violence and Prophecy by Caradoc
(www.visionsofcaradoc.co.uk)

THROUGH FIELDS OF GOLD

A Pilgrimage from Berlin to Rome

Tom Davies

First published in Great Britain 2000
Society for Promoting Christian Knowledge
Holy Trinity Church
Marylebone Road
London NW1 4DU

British Library Cataloguing-in-Publication Data

A catalogue record for this book is available from the British Library
ISBN 0-281-05358-8 (cased)
ISBN 0-281-05293-X (paper)

Typeset by Pioneer Associates, Perthshire
Printed in Great Britain by
Mackays of Chatham

Contents

The route of the pilgrimage

CHAPTER 1

Bedlam in Berlin

I drove my camper off the ferry in Calais late in the afternoon feeling full of sunshine and optimism which quickly turned into darkness and pessimism when I lost my way and realized I was soon going to be out of petrol. Quite why this happens with such regularity I'm never sure but one minute I know exactly what I'm doing and doing it and the next everything goes pear-shaped and I'm up some dark lane just sitting there, scratching my head and looking at a map with lots of curtains twitching and many eyes regarding me suspiciously.

All I knew for sure was that night had fallen and I was somewhere in Belgium where, after another small cruise around looking for signs, I pulled up in the car park of a football ground and drew my curtains. I needed a long sleep to get myself together so I thought I might try a little glug of wine to help me settle down in the arms of Morpheus. I had a nice bottle of wine all right but the trouble was I could not find the corkscrew even though I ransacked virtually the whole of my food cupboard like a dog frantically trying to locate his favourite bone.

At the beginning of any journey like this you are a blind man trying to find a routine. Within a routine you can move around without even thinking but, for the moment, it was all quite hopeless. I didn't know where the coffee was, the water tap had given up on me yet again and part of my sleeping bag was wet with something foul. And I badly needed that corkscrew. In desperation I picked up my Bible and asked for a verse. 'Why, oh Lord, do you stand so far off?' the Psalmist wanted to know. 'Why do you hide yourself in times of trouble?' Well that was a good one for me in my present state. And while I'm at it, why do you always keep me getting lost? Why has my water tap broken down yet again? Where have you hidden my corkscrew? Why have you got it in for *me*?

As the Psalmist continued talking about his loneliness and despair; how he felt alienated from the whole of mankind I was right there by his side. I could even picture this pained scholar sitting with a large hand spread over his forehead and a rumpled frown as he composed his lament on God's aloofness, sitting in some cave with a skull on his desk as his quill scratched the papyrus. I had travelled down the years and become as one with the Psalmist: we were brothers in rejection and despair, calling out to God to be a little kinder to us and stop hiding his face when there was trouble at mill.

A strange image cropped up that night in my dream-littered sleep in that damp sleeping bag. It was of a large blue and silver fish standing on its head deep in the sea and just outside the mouth of a cave. I knew what that was about as soon as I awoke. It was a coelacanth, a fossil fish which was millions of years old and mainly found just off Madagascar. I had been listening to a radio dramatization of a book by Samantha Weinberg about this fish the week before. When they finally found the fish it had been standing on its head outside a cave and I remember thinking that the image was funny, extraordinary and beautiful.

I knew then that I had to find my own coelacanth on my pilgrimage to the eternal city. This coelacanth would represent the object of my pilgrimage and, when I did finally catch up with it, whatever it was, all I knew for certain was that it absolutely had to be standing on its head.

But the weather the next morning might have been the

reward for a generation of fervent prayer because when I got up, the Belgian sky was bright with harvest festival sunshine and I was besieged by a bout of twittering optimism as I shaved in my driving mirror watched only by a gardener sweeping up leaves. This sunny brilliance continued on the road to Brussels and I felt at one with everything there is, driving through big, blue skies with the road unwinding beneath my feet and the cars and trucks whizzing all around. Summer and autumn were now on the cusp but already the fields had their arms full of autumn things – the gathered corn was lying about in giant chopped-up Swiss rolls, many of the fields were but shorn stubble and the first of the leaves were falling slowly from the trees. Most of the sunflowers had lost their leaves with their black faces all stooped like prisoners of war awaiting execution. In other fields the headless sunflower stalks bent this way and that, executed already.

But this golden munificence was extremely short-lived since I made the dramatic mistake of heading directly into the heart of Brussels instead of taking the ring road. This mistake was all the more grave since I hadn't actually *needed* to go into Brussels but decided on a whim that I would like to take a quick look at the new European Parliament building there. The long and the short of it was that I followed the traffic down one exhaust-filled tunnel then another then another and there soon came a point when I thought I'd never see daylight again. Breathing down there wasn't much fun either as I turned this way and that until I got onto some sort of underground ring road which I followed for an hour or so until I went down another endless tunnel. I did once spot a sign saying European Parliament but I never saw the place since I was back down another tunnel. Or perhaps it was the same tunnel I had first gone down. It was Kafka all the way although I can see these tunnels are probably a suitable metaphor for what's going on in the parliament above. I later met a woman who said she had a sister in Brussels and she still didn't know her way around all those tunnels and she had been living there for two years.

It would have been a big help if someone explained to the Belgians how helpful road signs can be. They should be told about arrows too. The French have great signs, good roads and know about arrows. Even the Spanish know about arrows even if they like to grow flowers and vines over them. But the one Brussels sign I did spot with an arrow pointing to Liège – where I more or less wanted to get to – abruptly changed to Lucid or something equally improbable and that confused me for another hour. Aix-La-Chapelle, I was also told later, actually has three different names scattered at random around Brussels, all clearly put there to add to visitors' growing fear and confusion.

At one point I stopped and asked a woman for directions to Liège but, as it turned out, she sent me the wrong way. What's the matter with these people? I mean to say, shouldn't they consider that we actually got Hitler off their backs and that it is simply no longer funny to send foreigners the wrong way? And the roads were a complete mess too with cracks and bits of tyres everywhere. A few brushes and a bit of filler wouldn't come amiss either.

I did eventually get out of those infernal tunnels, after losing one perfectly good morning of my life down them, although I am convinced there are drivers who have been down there for weeks. And now, on calm reflection, it seems to me that there are all those bureaucrats busy passing laws about how long our cucumbers should be or else putting a ban on perfectly good Welsh beef and there they were standing on top of one of the most monstrous torture chambers ever invented. Those tunnels are an affront to civilization and if the Brussels Parliament ever wants to do anything really useful they should pass an Act ensuring that all those tunnels should be blocked up with concrete and that, in future, all the locals should travel about on bicycles. I for one would sooner by-pass the whole of Belgium rather than take a chance on getting lost down there again.

After that nightmare in the tunnels of Brussels I decided I needed a proper bed with *dry* sheets to regain my balance – as well as a shower because I was beginning to pong worse than a charity clothes shop – so, after crossing the German border, I signed into one of those new Formula One Hotels, a chain which is mainly based in France. This is very much the kind of place a modern pilgrim, with his eye on his pocket, might seek out. You pay about £13 for one room in which there is a double bed, a bunk bed and a television. You rent this room for the night and, within reason, can put as many in there as you like. The showers and lavatories are along the landing and you can pretty much stay in these places without seeing anyone at all since all you need to do is put your credit card into a machine in the foyer – *with the black strip face down* – and you receive a code number which you use as a door key. You just punch the code into the door lock and, in the morning, you help yourself to breakfast in the tiny restaurant and get on your way. Forget about the fellowship of The Road in a Formula One then.

I had a nice chat with the manager, who once cooked in a Cardiff pub, before going off to take a shower and climb into bed where I hoped for the sleep of the dead. The trouble was a group of youths were having a party in the room directly above me and, after listening to their noise for more than an hour, I got up, packed my bag and jumped into my camper where I drove to the next village. I drew my curtains in the square and really did have the sleep of the dead. Once a tramp always a tramp, I guess.

The morning sounds of this small German village woke me – first the barking of a dog and then a distant cockerel. A car started and drove past and there was a throaty warbling, possibly of some doves. I peeped out and saw lots of house martins fluttering around the rooftops, and an old man who had been walking slowly down the pavement stopped to look at me before walking on again. The square itself was quietly warming up with the promise of nascent sunshine and no one had yet got the hump with me for sleeping outside their doorstep, which was encouraging.

I went back to the Formula One for the breakfast I had paid for. The manager said he'd had a few guests who had left early in his time but no one had yet come back for breakfast. Well, I'm Welsh and we're very careful about money, I told him. I'm also a writer who began his career with nothing and still has plenty of it left. I have also seen the inside of more hotel rooms than Gideon's Bible and, as I drove away from there, I really did hope it would be my last.

It was strange driving along the clean German autobahn after the mucky roads of Belgium. Most of the road was surrounded by thick forests with blackened tree trunks which thrummed under blue Fatherland skies. But you saw immediately that this was a society in love with speed by the way all the Mercs, BMWs and Audis went zipping down the outside lane at speeds in excess of 120 mph as if the whole of the Iraqi army was hot on their tails.

I was happy to plod along the inside, slow lane at a sedate 50 mph even if this made the lorry drivers less than happy since they were forever beeping me or waving their fists in frustration for me to get out of the way. This frustration became even more furious in the tunnels since there is something about a tunnel – perhaps after the trauma of getting lost in that labyrinth in Brussels – which makes me go even slower. Then the lorries got right up my backside and gave me a full blast on their air horns, a sound which was even more terrifying when it was amplified by the tight acoustics of a tunnel. Some of these lorries travel in tight convoys which are 20- or 30-strong and the insides of some of those tunnels can become as dark, wild jungles what with the maddened hisses of the air brakes, the black, poisonous puffs of the diesel exhausts and the shrill baboon screams of grinding gears. All those huge engines were roaring for the release of the open road again: the chance to race back out into the empty savannah of the autobahn and run wild.

A few lorries harassed me so much I thought I might be in a re-make of that film *Duel* but I soon began to learn to ignore them and, if they were in such a hurry, to let them get around me as best they could. I took the inside lane and held onto it grimly even if, as I was approaching Berlin, I looked down and to my mild amazement actually passed something.

The driver was an interesting-looking blonde and she was in a Trabant, one of those motorized lawnmowers once so beloved of the Communist bloc and which, it was said, was the only car in the world which always came off the worst after it had hit a pedestrian. It was also a major pollutant, disgorging five times more carbon monoxide and nine times more hydrocarbons than the average car. I gave the blonde a friendly little toot but she clearly thought I was taking the mickey out of her little car and replied by giving me the finger.

The thing about the autobahn, I soon discovered, was that it was almost completely being dug up rather like the rest of Germany in its bid for complete unification following the collapse of the Wall. In Wales we usually repair a few miles of road until the budget runs out and then leave it for the next year. Here they seemed to be tearing up the whole lot in one go, with heavy-duty earth-moving equipment and dumper trucks moving around everywhere. This was a society which clearly knew where it was going and wanted to get there fast. They should abandon the eagle and make the country's national emblem a dumper truck.

I had never visited Germany before and was feeling apprehensive. They had never been my favourite people, especially on holiday when they really did always nick the sun loungers around the pool before anyone else, and I kept recalling they had once set out to kill me and very nearly succeeded. The last war had been so real for me I might even have fought in it myself. One of my very first memories as a child was of sitting with my mother wrapped in shawl on the cellar stairs during an air raid. Also, a few years back, they were renovating my old house in Cardiff where, after pulling out the fire grate in my bedroom, they found an unexploded bomb which had fallen straight down the throat of the chimney and just lodged itself right there next to my bed. The bomb squad had to be called. So virtually all my youth I had slept within a few feet of an unexploded German bomb and I have long thought there must be a moral in that little story but for the life of me I have been totally unable to decide what it might be.

There was also another rough edge to this particular pilgrimage since my relationship with God had not been all that good of late and I had lost the practice of regular prayer. The pattern of our relationship over many years seemed to be long periods when everything was fine and relaxed followed perhaps by a period of bitterness, anger or even exhaustion. But then it would often come together again – often better than before – when he might speak to me either in quiet conversation or even violent vision.

Yet we had now been going through a period of coldness and sterility with one barely speaking to the other. I might feel him around but it was nothing to write home about, possibly because I'd been through a couple of mad years myself which began with a heart by-pass operation and ended up with me standing for the new Welsh Assembly for the Celtic Alliance, a party I had founded myself, specifically to invigorate the Welsh arts, and which received 220 votes, the lowest of any party in the election. Wales is generally not a good country to try and start any sort of revolution unless it' s a Red one.

You need to be alone and anchored to speak with God and he to you, I believe. You need to be far from the clamour of politics and my campaign had clearly shown me how positively un-Christian, if not downright irreligious, the whole thing can be, involving, as it does, the constant projection of yourself and the persistent manipulation of the media to further the cause of your own bloated ego. Ideas or ideals never seem to quite get in on the act, and more than ever I had learned that politicians are really little more than two-legged self-publicity machines.

So I was rather hoping this lone pilgrimage would fan some flames back into my faith again; that we would look out for and enjoy one another again. In faith, I believe, you enter into a direct, personal relationship with God which is then as rich and creative as you want to make it. But it does need work. And a bit of luck.

So here I was in a land I had grown to fear on a pilgrimage in which I was hoping to revive my faith. It also didn't help, I guessed, that I was making this journey in a camper van like a gypsy in a society not exactly famous for its tolerance of minorities. After my operation I also wasn't as strong as I had been. So it looked as if it was going to be a hard road, one which D. H. Lawrence called a 'savage pilgrimage'. Could I become good friends with God again? Well, clearly it might work if I set out to try and make this pilgrimage a journey along the wilder shores of faith; if I could open my heart to him and we could find one another again somewhere along The Road. This would make it a fruitful pilgrimage but, otherwise, I was surely going to find out quite how savage one pilgrimage could be.

I turned right at Spandau and accelerated down into the high, wide streets leading to central Berlin. Huge wheels of sunshine were rolling over the noisy traffic and still, golden canals. Berliners used to call this Führer weather – the warm sunshine they believed always broke through whenever Hitler appeared.

The rhythms of the city became more jangled and there were huge eruptions of mechanical noise on almost every corner. I once worked in Manhattan and had always thought that place throbbed with pure energy but even that fevered anthill had little on this because here *everything* seemed to be being torn down or built up – and all at the same time. Jack-hammers pounded away on the roads. Careful now, mind that cable, go up this one way and, with a little luck, you can get out on another. Ah, another long tailback. Squeegee merchants danced around the stationary traffic although they clearly thought my windscreen was too big to tackle.

Even as you looked at the skyline it seemed to be changing before your very eyes, from the massive self-confidence of Norman Foster's massive cupola on top of the Reichstag to the high, thin spire of the Television Tower and the soaring glass cathedral of the new Sony headquarters. SEE YOU TOMORROW, it said on the top floor as yet more sheets of glass rose up into the air like departing souls. Another dumper truck came reversing out of a yard, exhaust fumes belching dragon-like.

The pavements streamed with people – young men jabbering animatedly into mobile phones, effeminate men with dogs and handbags, suicidal kids on bikes and skate boards, old women with faces which had clearly seen too much and some achingly beautiful women with a curious aura of melancholy about them. Interspersed through all this was the usual street riff-raff – the sellers of silver rings and frankfurters, the quick-draw caricaturists and pavement artists, the needy beggars, the clowns done up as outsize dolls . . . the whole gaudy street cabaret which, fascinating as it was, never quite seemed to detract from the pulverizing building work going on all around.

The Wall – perhaps the most hated wall in the world – came down about ten years ago and when it did you could just see a massed band of architects, engineers and builders all throwing their hats into the air as they looked over at the huge, grey tenements of East Berlin, shouting: 'Ah, at last something we can really get our teeth stuck into.' This is a race born to build: their energy is both fantastic and ferocious. I was also beginning to understand how they were once so good at destroying things. Hitler could never once have considered that he would fail with a people as positively rampant as this behind him.

I always like to visit zoos and found an interesting clue to the German personality while walking around Berlin Zoo, and it came when I was watching some toddlers playing in a sandpit there. Now whereas you and I, as children, might have put a coin in a little train which lit up or a horse which rocked up and down, the little Helmuts here – for there were no girls in that sandpit – put small coins into small bulldozers and tractors which they could then operate to move huge piles of sand around to their hearts' content. It would seem Germans never put away childish things when they became men because they were never given childish things in the first place.

There is little left of the Wall except for a thin row of cobbles which follows its original line through this large building site and one lonely wooden watchtower standing in the middle of a forest of cranes. You can now walk freely where there were once savage dogs, mines and automatically tripped machine guns. About a hundred yards of the Wall has been retained to form the basis of a new museum but, in an amusing historical irony, this remaining section has been fenced off to protect it from visitors' chisels.

They are also planning to build a new Chapel of Reconciliation on the site of the old Church of Reconciliation on this 'death strip' which the Communists famously blew up on 22 January 1985 'in order to raise the security, order and integrity of the national border to West Berlin'. Federal Chancellor Helmut Kohl said this event was a symbol of how difficult it was going to be to overcome the division of Germany. The parish bade farewell to its church with speeches and dances on the Wall. People spoke of their powerlessness but nevertheless the Wall came down a few years later.

The parish has since managed to rescue the bells and the old altar of the church so the new architects will build on the ruins, returning the altar to its original location. The new walls will be built from bare clay with a wooden roof but the interesting attitude throughout this new design, I think, is the modern German attitude to confront terror and not turn their backs on it and try to forget. Forgetting is, after all, easier than remembering, is it not? There's always less pain to deal with when you simply forget. And another aspect to this attitude, I found, was in their curious unwillingness to cover the past up. This wasn't being forced on them at gun-point; they wanted to do it for themselves.

I always read Visitors' Books when I visit any sort of shrine, usually to look for any English comments, and here, in the Exhibition Centre about the Wall, I found a host of rabidly racist remarks – *Hitler had it right. He should have killed a lot more Jews* – which there had been no attempt to expunge.

Later, in Colditz, I found a rather nasty row in English on one page of the Visitors' Book which again no one had made any attempt to remove. A woman had complained there hadn't been enough information in English there. *So why don't you learn German, you old bitch,* another had written. *I say, this isn't cricket,* some old colonel had then chimed in. *Let's not have a silly quarrel like this.* You'd think they'd at least tear these pages out. They certainly would have done so in Wales. But, oh no, there it was for all to see and it all suggested a rather unusual self-confidence which enabled them to face a shady past and a sticky present and live with it.

There was a little excitement at the time of my visit since it had been reported that construction workers had uncovered part of Adolf Hitler' s wrecked bunker. Work on a new street had turned over a massive concrete block, clearly part of the New Reich chancellery where Hitler had killed himself on 30 April 1945. The Red Army had blown up the bunker and filled the remains with sand.

It had also just been revealed that Hitler's bones had been secretly burned at night about 25 years ago. The remains were then tipped into the sewers of Magdeburg, a city then in the old Communist German Democratic Republic (GDR). They had been sent there in 1946 but later destroyed since the Russians feared they would one day be discovered and the site turned into a shrine to Hitler. They still have his skull stored away somewhere in Moscow, however, in a small cardboard box originally used for ballpoint pen refills.

Later I lingered outside Checkpoint Charlie, half expecting Richard Burton to come rolling up out of the fog. YOU ARE ENTERING THE AMERICAN SECTOR, a sign said. THE CARRYING OF WEAPONS IS FORBIDDEN. Some of the Communist buildings of the old GDR are still empty after ten years, one man told me, since most of them have been contaminated with asbestos. But they'll get around to them next week for sure. Your eyes move one way and another. That's where the Nazi Party once burned all the forbidden books and, if you look down that window, you will see a library with bare shelves. Nothing was moving around the Brandenburg Gate – yet another traffic jam.

I did find one place of refuge in this huge open-air building site and that was in the 3-square kilometre Tiergarten where you can actually glory in the space and silence only trees can bring. The Berlin noise barely penetrates this park and, when the city became too much and my legs were on the point of revolt, I would sit on a bench in there, letting the dappled sunlight and the solidity of the trees feed directly into my frazzled bloodstream. The trees grew all around saying nothing except tree talk, the breezes occasionally picking up all the leaves and making them chatter excitedly.

Germans clearly love their trees and I knew how they must have felt when they complained of missing the German forests when they were away on the huge, bare steppes fighting the 'mad dogs' of Russians in the battle for Stalingrad. I had just been reading Antony Beevor's book on the battle and this had been one of the recurring complaints in their letters to their loved ones back home. A butterfly fluttered past me which, in religious art, always represented the resurrection. A few autumnal leaves fell slowly just near a stream, falling on the moving water and sailing away fast.

And it was about then in a clearing in the Tiergarten, where water met sunlight, that I saw the swift and sudden image of a hand holding up a sheet of paper to a door and another hand holding a hammer and nailing the paper to the door in ringing, metallic blows. The hands were strong and the fingers thick as these blows echoed and re-echoed through the listening trees until they faded away into the sunshine and silence from where they had come. The image of those hammering hands, at once so faint and yet so strong, made me sit up with a start. I knew then – just knew – that God had begun talking to me again and that this was indeed going to be a fruitful pilgrimage in which we were going to explore one another's natures.

There were no campsites in central Berlin and, unwilling to chance rubbing up the *Polizei* the wrong way, with their big machine guns, by camping wild next to their sacred Reichstag, I signed into a pension near Zoo station. But the place was nightmarish, full of drunks and people running up and down the corridors in the middle of the night. My room had flock wallpaper and gilt light fittings such as you might have found in a Bradford curry house. Bare wires poked threateningly from the walls and the carpet stuck to my bare feet. The television was showing a blizzard of static on every channel and, to make matters worse, my room was next to the restaurant one side and the lavatory for the whole of the landing on the other. A ghostly moaning, which might have been something to do with the central heating, went on all night and an extremely hostile insect managed to work in a few good bites on my leg before I could manage a good smack on its head.

I checked out more in need of a good night's sleep than

when I checked in and fully and finally resolved never to sign into a hotel again. But my stay in that pension was fortunate in one sense because it meant I discovered the nearby Kaiser Wilhelm Memorial Church which I knew, as soon as I looked at it, would make an interesting, formal start for my pilgrimage from Berlin to Rome. It didn't make any sense at first and I couldn't quite understand why a ruined church had been left in the middle of Berlin. The old church had been destroyed in air-raids in 1943, I was to learn, and it was not until 1956 that a competition was launched to design a new one. After a passionate public debate the winning design put a new church around the old ruin. They didn't even repair the blasted spire and so set up an interesting link between the old and new, between war and peace and between love and hate. As you wander around the outskirts of this confusing complex, noting the blown-out windows and bomb scars in the masonry, you wonder how the thing stays up at all until you see that the new buildings actually support it. Berliners call the church the 'hole in the tooth' or the 'powder box and lipstick'. So we've got that admirable willingness to take hold of the past again; to hold it up and say: 'Yes, we did all that for sure but we are *not* going to do it again.'

They were selling apples in the vestry and, when I went inside, I found a circular, darkened nave almost surrounded by a solid sea of blue stained glass which the sinking Berlin sun was striking vivaciously. There are 21,292 panes of this blue glass, it said in my guide book. 'I wish that my house may always remain open so that those in need of consolation in this tormented city may find it here at any hour,' said the architect. 'And I wish, for myself and for all of us that the shadow of terror will never be cast again through the dream of light from this glass.'

On the altar the golden figure of Christ glowed like the light of the resurrection set in the darkness of death. I also spotted a moving charcoal drawing of the Madonna of Stalingrad, done by a clergyman and doctor, Kurt Reuber, when the Germans were trapped outside Stalingrad in 1942. A copy of this drawing has been sent, as a gesture of reconciliation, to Coventry Cathedral which was also ravaged by the bombs of war. For their part, Coventry sent this church a Cross of Nails taken from the burned-out rafters of their own cathedral. Each Friday the Litany of Reconciliation is prayed at this Cross of Nails in Berlin while it is also being prayed in Coventry.

So here I was, then, beginning my own European pilgrimage in the autumn of 1999. This was far from being the most beautiful church I have ever prayed in but her eerie inner tensions and the way she appeared to be reaching out across the world seemed to accurately reflect my own worries and concerns about war and peace, love and hate and how and in what way God was still moving through his lost and fallen world. I looked up and around at this amazing sea of blue stained glass, trying to draw strength from this oasis of calm in the middle of the hurly burly of Berlin. You can often pick up on the presence of years of healing prayer in churches like this but, in such a schizophrenic atmosphere, I kept picking up on a series of quandaries. There was a sense of puzzled prayer in here although, to add to the puzzle, I wasn't at all sure if it was in the church or actually inside me. Perhaps Germany remains the land of big questions, almost more than any other, and I wondered then whether I would find even the smallest answers in the shifting dreams of light in all that blue glass.

CHAPTER 2

A Chapel of Escapes

My eyes opened onto a huge meadow of golden mist in Wittenberg. The dew on the newly mown grass was so thick you could wash your face in it and, as the rising sun continued to break through the mist, my mouth picked up the clear taste of autumn. The morning air even gave the leaf mould an unusually fresh edge and the fanned leaves on a nearby chestnut tree had gone wrinkled and brown. A thick bank of nettles had already died.

I stepped out into the mist glorying in the pure light of this resurrection dawn. The dew had also gathered in glittering groups of tears in the cobwebs where it looked as if the spiders didn't walk their gossamer tightropes until the sun had dried them out. A gang of blackbirds were already up and about their day, all fluttering one way and then suddenly wheeling about and flying back into themselves. Quite how they didn't actually knock one another out when they did this only a blackbird could know for sure.

A path took me down to the bank of a huge river, flowing silently and with yet more pockets of golden mist on it like a scattered conclave of fabulously wealthy ghosts. A man was fishing on the opposite bank and I spotted the tail of a field mouse as it hurried through the damp grass. Mornings simply didn't get minted with more promise than this since, directly behind me, a huge church spire rose, black on gold, above the trees. That spire might even be the most famous in all Christendom and, if not that, then the church certainly had the most famous door.

A bell rang out over the meadow making me feel even more worshipful. This was a quiet and intimate moment with God for sure: a time when our heartbeats became as one on this the first golden morning of the rest of my life. A hot-air balloon floated above the trees on the other side of the river: a dark round avatar floating on a sea of misty gold.

At such moments, full with heavenly fragrances and with the very air vibrating silently like some giant angelic generator, we can twist one of Martin Luther's brilliant metaphors and say that our wickedness is clothed in the merits of Christ. Our sins have been concealed from the awesome gaze of God as we stand alone in an autumnal field glorying in the truth and promise of our faith. This pilgrimage was going well: we were already getting on together better than ever before.

People, mostly students, I guessed, were waiting for the train at Wittenberg station as I pressed a button on a level crossing to be allowed back into the town. A sea captain had told me about that sacred meadow the night before when I had asked him to suggest somewhere interesting where I could sleep. He had clearly picked up on the spirit of my pilgrimage since I couldn't remember when I had last awoken in such an enchanted place. But it *had* taken ages to actually find that level crossing button in the dark.

An atmosphere of medieval calm pervaded the central square of the town which, with its cobblestones and old houses, was as you might have expected it to be in the time of the old reformer. This calm was also completely at odds with the grey, smelly geometry of the fertilizer and rubber industries which you first see as you drive in. Nasty, drainy niffs, possibly from these factories, often rode the winds. Up until ten years ago, until the fall of the Wall, Wittenberg was but another outpost of the old GDR.

Many of the shops and offices around the square were already open – Salamander, Commerzbank, Kaufhaus – and another bell rang out as an old lady on failing legs and with a walking stick stumbled past the small open-air stalls selling flowers and fruit. You wondered what those old legs had stumbled through in their time, what social outrages those eyes had witnessed under the Reds. But there would be nothing to upset her on this resurrection morning.

Doctor Martinus joined me as I walked down the pavement towards the castle church; a bulky, short figure of about 5ft 2ins, with a bull-neck and a bold pugnacious face, not really handsome in any formal sense and with short, grey hair. He had been putting on a lot of weight lately, largely through drinking too much beer. His wife hadn't been too thrilled about his intake and had been nagging him about it a bit. His body had also been prey to many crippling illnesses which included angina, dropsy, piles, a kidney stone and mysterious swellings of the muscles. Beer helped him to live with it all, he often told his wife. But she wasn't convinced.

We walked together past an antiquarian bookshop and a ladies' clothes shop with lots of frilly French underwear in the window. Students with their satchels bulging with books rode past on bicycles. The streets were largely litter-free although there were the usual drifts of fag-ends. If nothing else, the Communists certainly managed to teach everyone to smoke.

It would be difficult to picture Wittenberg in his time when he occupied that famous pulpit here. Then the town consisted of a few hundred clay houses with thatched roofs. The place was also overrun by a plague of mice and they had their own special place of public execution. The streets were also thick with churned-up mud, making walking difficult particularly as some of the townsfolk shamelessly bared themselves and relieved themselves in public – a habit which provoked another bout of his pulpit ire.

A time of medieval superstition and darkness then in which

this deeply emotional man sought to shine a light of reason as he carefully pastored his flock while also angrily attacking the corruption of Rome. But nothing was that simple about this complex man. He was prey to depression and felt himself to be suffused with sin. He even called his every fart a sin. 'Now sad, now sickly, now happy, now depressed,' he wrote of himself.

He was humming a hymn to himself when we came to the door of the castle church to which he once so gloriously nailed his 95 theses attacking the sale of indulgences and serving notice on the Pope that the days of corruption of the Catholic Church were over. The primacy of scriptural authority over church tradition was one of his key ideas which he promoted by a sort of popular journalism. He spoke directly to the people and fully understood the power of modern publicity. He even used crude cartoons to show the difference between papal and primitive Christianity but his main method of evangelism was through pamphlets and books. He was the first media celebrity, the first to bask in mass appeal and his thoughts became the talk of every German town. In a sense that nailing of the theses to this church door was the first great publicity stunt and, if it didn't happen – as some have suggested – it was an even better publicity stunt. Not that he could do that today since the old wooden door has long been burned down and replaced by a bronze door with the theses printed on it in Latin.

Brother Martinus actually began framing his independent theology here, making Wittenberg one of the great universities of Europe even if many of his contemporaries persisted in calling the town 'a hole'.

We entered the church through the other door and I was immensely pleased I had met him at last. This was a man with a great mind which often danced with important new insights. But first and foremost, he was a man like you and me. He never strutted about the town with his feet in a ditch and his head in a cloud of piety. This was a street-wise man who could punch his weight and was always prepared to listen to ordinary people; someone who believed in the value of music, beer and laughter; someone who did not advocate literacy merely that people could read the Bible but because he wanted them to read *everything*. Yes, yes, he was a man, just like you and me . . .

'Avoid sorrow however you are,' he once wrote. 'Except for manifest sins I hereby absolve you of all merriments wherein you may seek comfort, be it eating, dancing, gaming, whatever.'

He was also one of the first to support the emancipation of women, not only encouraging one group to flee a nunnery near Grimma but ending up marrying one of them who, many suspect, then ended up becoming the power behind the throne. 'No sweeter thing than the love of a woman,' he wrote. 'May a man be so fortunate.' Fatherhood was the supreme earthly joy and this most human of men even recommended sexual fantasy as a way of overcoming the blues. Children were not the sole object of making love, he said, a good point which again didn't fill the Pope with too much happiness when he heard it.

There was also one issue on which we were absolutely united and that was the inscrutable mystery of the mind of God. Rationality was not one of God's special qualities, he believed, although he admired it in man, saying that was what made him apart from animals. God did 'proper' and 'strange' works, he thought; you never really knew what was on his mind or anything about his motives and I was right there with him on that.

An organ was playing in the castle church as we walked down the aisle and a youth was polishing the pews. Sunshine smashed against the stained glass as busts of other Protestant reformers like Knox and Wycliffe looked on.

His grave was on the right-hand side of the altar with a single white rose in a brown earthenware jug standing directly in front of it. The grave was still, but you could still sense the tempestuous fury which had once exploded out of that pulpit right there; a fury of hot passion and diamond words which had swirled up out of this small German town and then blown everywhere to change the shape of the world forever.

But there was no fury coming out of that pulpit that morning as we both stood there looking down on where he lay in his pauper's coffin; just a smiling, nodding calm at a life fulfilled. I wanted to take his hand or hold him in my arms and say, 'Well done.' But a group of chattering schoolchildren walked up to the altar and the Great Reformer disappeared in a splash of stained glass light.

Wittenberg now attracts some 2,000 tours a year and they sell 100,000 nights of accommodation. And they have all come just as I have come: to find out a little more about the great man and perhaps try and discover what actually shaped the thunder and lightning of his personality. He is still very much alive in these parts. Each year in June they celebrate his wedding – that of the rebel priest to the runaway nun – with three days of medieval music, juggling and mime together with parades with horse-drawn carts and a re-enactment of the wedding itself.

A new Lutheran centre is also being set up here – there are five million Lutherans in America alone – and I had a chat with the affable boss there, Dean Bard, still busy putting everything into place. He came here long after the fall of the Wall – even if he'd always had a long-term love affair with Germany – and we talked a lot about the way the Holy Spirit played an active part in the Wall's destruction; something I was later to learn even more about in Leipzig. 'The church was the one social institution free of government control,' he said. 'It became a gathering place for dissent, somewhere where you could actually come and talk freely about Communism. We became the focus of the growing unease with the Wall and the Holy Spirit did the rest.'

I picked up a back-packing hitch-hiker after leaving Wittenberg who, almost needless to report, was an Australian. I don't know what it is about Australians but, when they get to a certain age, all they want to do is go walkabout rather like their native Aborigines. I have always fancied they must have been fed with big lumps of concentrated wanderlust when they were babies or that they were given bus passes and ferry tickets for their birthdays instead of toys or toilet soaps like the rest of us.

Whatever, they were up and off having barely got out of the pram and, if you cross any desert or explore the darkest jungle, you will usually come across a huge back-pack being trundled along by a pair of muscular Aussie legs. But for all their physical panache they are not always very interesting. They know hundreds of tales of The Road, which are rather like dirty jokes you have mostly heard before, and they generally don't like talking about ideas or anything else that comes in words of more than one syllable.

This one was so boring he could have put a glass eye to sleep, going on about the 'sheilas and grog' of the nightlife in Berlin which is of no particular interest to me because I have long given up nightlife anywhere. He was also – surprise, surprise – making his way to Katmandhu and, after a few more miles of this, I couldn't stand it anymore and told him to get out. Always remember there is nothing at the end of the road – particularly if that road is going to Katmandhu – I wanted to tell him. But I didn't. Perhaps he'll find out for himself but he was so dull I wouldn't hold my breath.

It was 9 a.m. and the clock struck dully as I sat on a bench in front of the university in the huge square of Augustusplatz in Leipzig. The square rose directly up to embrace the bare, empty sky with little cluttering the crouching cityscape. Even the large fountain seemed subdued except a dog had now got in there and was occasionally letting out yelps of pure happiness as he rolled around in the spray. Car tyres puttered softly across the cobbles and every so often an electric tram whined past. In fact it was only the trams which emphatically broke up the eerie silence of this square where just a few pigeons marauded around looking for something interesting to eat.

Directly behind me was a huge black sculpture with the face of Lenin surrounded by other heroes of the revolution all ready for another hard day's night down on the collective. This place was once a church until the Communists did what they usually did with churches and blew it up, later putting the university here. Leipzig, until ten years ago, was one of the great industrial centres of the GDR.

Further down towards the heart of the shopping centre the first waves of the Saturday crowds were moving through the newly opened department stores and open-air flower stalls selling giant sunflowers and roses. A man with a fag in his mouth was cooking frankfurters and a girl on stilts was flinging a diabolo up and down with not a little skill. You had to grant that many of these young Germans were really beautiful with their fine cheekbones, blue eyes and legs that went on forever. And that was just the boys. Intrepid skateboarders were doing stunts on stone steps that I couldn't even do on my own two feet and there were besuited businessmen with beer-gut bellies, several young American Mormons up and about looking for converts and a gang of purple-haired punks with ragged stockings and pins through their lips. I'm Not A Racist – I Hate Everyone, one of the T-shirts said. Deutschland Skinheads, said another.

An opera singer, clearly a professional on hard times, was singing into a microphone in front of a bank with a cassette player providing the musical accompaniment. He had a fine voice and stood there magnificently, with his back erect and looking around him imperiously, mopping his brow with a handkerchief with slow and exaggerated care. In fact he had soon attracted quite a crowd as he sang about his lost love or how broke he was and how thrilling it would be for all concerned if the populace flung a huge amount of marks into his hat. Luther had one of his famous disputations with Johannes Eck just up the road. Eck was a hardline Papist who believed that Rome was the centre of the world and used all his remorseless polemics to try and cut Luther down to size. As if. There's a famous portrait of Luther by the artist Lucas Cranach, when he was on the run and known as Junker Gorg, in the museum directly opposite our warbling opera singer.

I enjoyed Leipzig from the start, particularly the serenity of the streets and those whining trams. The shopping arcades and bookshops were a joy too and you felt not too much had been knocked down here yet. A couple of young girls had even smiled at me as I sat there making notes and that didn't happen too often since the days when I was young and hard to get. I would have liked to have been a student here, I decided, dressed in black and much-fancied by all the girls as I talked wild-eyed rubbish about capitalism in the coffee bars. I might even have become a Stasi agent, since the secret police once recruited a lot of English students in Leipzig University, and could have ended up sending important information to Moscow and getting exchanged for Richard Burton in the Berlin fog at Checkpoint Charlie.

In fact I had come here in search of the story of that church tucked around that corner. It had a light brown rendering and a high octagonal tower with a golden weather vane on top. A church poster advertised an Orgel Konzert and one side of it was scaffolded. The interior was spacious with lots of overhanging balconies. Classical columns rose to the roof where they splayed out into palms. Pure light hung in the clear windows and on one side of the altar was yet another Cross of

Nails presented, as an act of conciliation, by Coventry Cathedral. A huge organ sat alone above the vestry and on the altar was a painting of an angel of peace. A drunken young man was causing some bother by stretching out on the pews. He didn't make any obvious sense because he was clearly not a derelict since he had lots of jewellery on his fingers and around his neck. But no one was actually doing anything about him even if a few men were keeping an eye on him from a discreet distance.

We were in the Nikolai Church where I met Antje Siebert, a young woman with a broad toothy smile and a brisk bird-like manner, who is training to be a Lutheran pastor here. At just 28 her life has encompassed many of the upheavals of modern Germany and she graciously told me at some length of how she had grown up in a Communist society and how, after much difficulty, she was finally won over to God. From other sources I have also managed to piece together the story of the Nikolai Church and the role it played in the downfall of the Wall.

Antje's father was a Lutheran reverend and, as a child in the Leipzig area, she went to Church and learned about Christianity. The Communists allowed you to be a Christian even if it was always frowned on and the Stasi listened to your every word on the telephone.

'I was the fourth child and I didn't speak about things in school that I did at home. It was compulsory to join the Free German Youth but I learned to live with the situation. I sang a lot in the youth choir and prayed a lot too. I also wanted to become a Communist Pioneer because I wanted a neckerchief like all the others. I also wanted the blue blouse of the German Youth. But, as it turned out, I managed to stay out of the Communist organizations and decided to study psychology at the University. A professor with very big eyes had once asked me if I wanted to study theology but I decided to stay put. Yet, in 1989, in my first year, things were stirring as never before. Loud denunciations were being made of the state. There were peace prayers in this church every Monday and I was warned to stay away. It was always packed in here and people were always being carted off to prison for protesting. One day there were so many they used the animal pounds of a visiting agricultural fair to lock them all up. But I wasn't a hero of Leipzig because, when things really got moving, the Communist Party sent me, along with the other students, to dig potatoes in Mecklenburg.'

It really must have been bliss to be alive in that Leipzig dawn just before the fall of the Wall. They had peace prayer meetings in the Nikolai week after week with a dedicated Monday evening service. At first only a small number attended but, if the Communists did anything unpopular, which they managed about three times a week, a lot more attended in protest. Soon this prayer momentum began to build and, if you didn't get here very early, you didn't get in at all and had to join the prayers in the squares and streets outside.

Arrests mounted. The Stasi attended every service, watched everyone and listened to every conversation. Both sides kept striking at one another in their own ways. More police vans rolled up and carted more people away. Every window ledge of this church was strewn with fresh flowers; every darkness was held up by a huge sea of glittering candles. Everyone was praying for freedom and peace with the words of the Beatitudes, those perennially inspiring lines of the Sermon on the Mount.

In May 1989 the police blocked all roads to the church with checkpoints and even closed them altogether when there were prayers for peace. More arrests or 'temporary detentions' followed and then came that momentous October when, for hours on end, uniformed police battered the people who made no attempt to defend themselves. Almost everyone knew in their hearts that the Communist Party was fatally wounded: the only real question was when would it actually die.

The Communist Party hit back blindly and stupidly, ordering its members to fill up the prayer meetings in the Nikolai. Church leaders like the Revd C. Führer seized the opportunity to preach the Word to them, telling them about truly revolutionary ideas like Blessed are the poor or Love your enemies or The first shall be last. Monday after Monday the Stasi, who had been attending from the beginning, together with the party members who had now been ordered here, heard these lines and what they meant to the world. The preachers were also always careful to insist that people stayed within the law and the call was always to non-violence. It was also seen as important to emphasize the solidarity between the church and the gospel in the threatening situation of those days.

When 2,000 people left the church on that night of 9 October they were greeted by tens of thousands outside all with candles in their hands. You need two hands to protect a candle flame from going out so it was not possible for anyone to carry stones or petrol bombs at the same time. Candles have a brightness and purity which are at the very heart of faith. They carry our prayers into the darkness long after we have stopped saying them. 'I am the light of the world,' said Christ.

A miracle was unfolding that night of candles and prayer in Leipzig. There was no violence of any kind and not one shop window had ever been broken throughout those weeks and months of dissent. Troops and police talked with the parishioners and then withdrew. The clean, sweet winds of the Holy Spirit were blowing through that extraordinary Leipzig night and who could doubt that one man in particular was moving through that praying, incandescent throng? He would have been walking around determinedly, exhorting all he came near with words of quiet encouragement; a man of about 5ft 2ins, with a bull-neck and pugnacious face, not really handsome in any way and with short, grey hair. Oh, for sure he would have been there all right; he would have been there in the middle of Augustusplatz urging his flock to show courage, defiance and love.

The Holy Spirit had indeed made yet another lightning strike and the Nikolai Church had been the willing and worthy conductor. A new wind had come straight from Calvary and, within a few weeks, both the Communist Party and an ideological dictatorship had been blown away. *You will succeed, not by military power or by your own strength but by my spirit, says the Lord. You will succeed . . .*

And so, when Antje Siebert came back from digging potatoes in Mecklenburg, everything had changed and a lot of closed doors had been opened. She married and now has a daughter. She met that professor 'with big eyes' again and he persuaded her to change from psychology to theology; she soon attained a degree. Now she is studying the art of the sermon and learning about church administration in Nikolai. She will become a Lutheran reverend like her father and then . . . Who knows? In this land of many quandaries and seismic political upheavals almost anything is possible.

Places of worship are many, varied and even strange, I have discovered on The Road, but I can't think of anywhere quite as strange as the chapel I found the next day in Colditz. I hadn't planned to go there since I was still in hot pursuit of the spirit of Martin Luther but, on the way to Erfurt, I spotted a sign to Colditz and thought I'd take a quick look around there, if only because the castle once formed the subject of a popular television series years ago in Britain.

I can still see myself now as a youngster, huddled in warm anticipation in front of the television . . . the creepy music, the low-angled shots of the high castle walls and all those

Hooray Henrys constantly plotting their escapes. But what was the real truth of the place? Well, I'd find out soon enough if I followed the sign.

The Saxony skies were overcast – which was something of a relief after so many days of brilliant sunshine – and an American-style swing band was entertaining an appreciative crowd of locals in the courtyard when I got inside. Stalls were selling food, beer, lace and musical instruments. Apparently it was a fête to raise funds for the castle which, after the war, had fallen into something of a forgotten limbo, not even appearing in guide books because the old GDR couldn't make any propaganda out of the place as they did remorselessly out of the concentration camps. So they simply moved Colditz off the map and left it to rot. As subtle as sledgehammers, those Communists.

Now in something of a state of disrepair, to put it mildly, there is a general desire, as in the rest of unified Germany, to tart the castle up and attract more visitors. Rather alarmingly, they want to put a restaurant in the old cells and have already got rid of the de-lousing shed. At least the Communists didn't seem to feel this burning need to tear everything down and start again.

This castle was once Oflag IVC, the Third Reich's most secure prisoner-of-war camp and, just looking up and around me as the band played Glenn Miller's *Little Brown Jug*, I could well imagine how all those prisoners' hearts must have sunk when they first arrived here and realized this was going to be their new home.

Straddling the top of a high hill and overlooking a river the outside walls are seven-feet thick and the seven-storey courtyard walls are more than 80ft high. There were also the medieval defences like the drawbridge to deal with and, by the time the Germans had placed barbed wire all around it, put in floodlighting which was kept lit all around the clock and placed listening devices in the walls every 30 feet or so, this was clearly a prison which meant business.

Men were only put in here who had tried to escape before and there were also usually more guards than prisoners. Nevertheless 300 were caught in escape attempts, 130 made it clear of the castle and 30 made it home. They escaped by wriggling through man-holes, disguising themselves as Rhine Maidens or piles of rubbish, hiding in waste-paper baskets or under bread vans. They were under orders to be a total nuisance to the enemy, orders they followed to the letter since they also picked every lock in sight, sawed workmen's ladders in half, pinched visiting dignitaries' hats, dropped water bombs on the guards, tied sheets together and, most crucially, were forever tunnelling down into the ground like so many demented moles desperate to get some red-hot party in the very centre of the earth.

As the swing band continued playing I looked up at all the surrounding grilled windows and could easily imagine the strained white faces of all the men who were once locked up here, looking down at me sadly and forlornly as they wondered if they would ever hold their loved ones in their arms again. You could also actually feel their very ghosts slippering all around you on the cobblestones, muttering behind their hands, plotting what to do next, who was going out tonight . . .

An exhibition dedicated to the exploits of these men has been opened in the castle tower with photographs of many of them and exhibits like the tennis racket with a compass in the handle, playing cards and chess sets which concealed maps, forged German banknotes and a typewriter which could be taken to bits to conceal it in the frequent searches of their cells. Most of the visitors to this exhibition are British, including some who were once locked up here.

But it was the chapel which I found the most interesting,

particularly after Herr Loffler, our guide, explained that this was where so many prisoners pretended to pray while they were actually trying to escape. At one time there must have been more holes under this chapel floor than in the mouldiest lump of gorgonzola and the place now looks pretty mouldy too with crumbling walls, tiered wooden dry-rot galleries and a huge pile of rusty barbed wire on the altar. Also the pulpit looked so tiny the preachers here must have been midgets since most normal men would have been hard pushed to get their left leg inside it.

Yet, in the opposite corner, behind some dusty pews, they have excavated a tunnel which, you can see with the aid of a light, went straight down through some ten feet of rock. This was the French tunnel which, in fact, went on for a further 30 yards and took 22 men eight months to dig. The electric supply for the tunnel lighting was run out of the sacristy and they even managed to enclose this 'illegal' cable inside a proper pipe. They also created so much rubble they had to carry it out inside their trousers in the time-honoured manner while also depositing a lot of it in the cavities in the eaves above the chapel. They even hid their escape clothes in the organ tubes.

When the guards did smell a rat – but weren't too sure – they tried to close the chapel but the French chaplain, Abbé Jean-Jean, protested that it must stay open so that he could properly teach the mysteries of faith. The chapel was positively the *only* place he could do this and so the Germans gave in. But when the guards heard some strange noises coming up out of the sewers one day they lowered a small boy on a rope down a 'suspicious' hole and the boy screamed out in terror when he all but landed on top of three filthy Frenchmen down there. The tunnel was soon filled up but the same French chaplain then distinguished himself further by going for a walk one day and disappearing into the woods. They caught him soon enough but the word was the Germans were no longer too keen on any continuing worship in that chapel and had developed a truly jaundiced, if not absolutely cynical eye on the role of Christianity in Colditz.

Yet this chapel was then to feature in what might have become the most spectacular escape attempt in man's long and restless inability to stay locked inside four walls. The British began building a full-scale glider behind a false wall in the attic above the chapel and it was hoped to launch two men on a flight out. They actually built this glider – The Cock of Colditz – out of wooden planks, the blue and white cotton of palliasses and many stinking buckets of glue. The whole operation was kept secret by an elaborate stooging system and the glider was never discovered by the Germans except for one guard – clearly a 100 carat cheapskate since his silence was bought for 500 Players cigarettes.

The glider was going to be launched off a ramp by a giant elastic band made from footballs and baseballs and the initial momentum was to be provided by a bath filled with concrete which was going to be dropped 60 feet through three floors and holes made especially for the event. An opening was also going to be made through the gable end wall on the night of the escape and it was hoped the glider would fly for five miles and land in a soft meadow whereupon the men would hop out and leg it as fast as they could go. Perhaps fortunately for those two men, then, the glider never made it into the air because the end of the war intervened. It was later destroyed although a miniature model is now on display in the exhibition.

I must say, the more I thought about it, the more I loved the notion of men pretending to pray while they were actually trying to escape since both dispositions are in essence the same, even if one is spiritual and the other physical. Both prayer and escape affirm man's most basic desire to lose his earthly shackles; both tell of the real need to be free.

In need of a shower I later signed into a campsite just

behind Colditz and managed to wash in at least seven seconds of hot water before my token ran out and it ran freezing cold. At least I had managed to wash the soap off unlike a German banker I met in there who had only managed to get himself fully lathered before his *two* tokens had run out. He then had to stand in the middle of the wash room and wipe himself down in front of a hand basin.

But he was jolly enough in the circumstances, rather like most of the other people I had met on this trip. In fact no one at all had so far upset me despite the clear provocation of my sleeping in the car parks of their football stadiums or on their sacred meadows. Not that I could so far claim much luck in feeling around the bumps on the head of the German personality. They seemed obsessively clean – often spending half an hour in the showers on the camp sites and then another half an hour primping and preening their bodies – even if a few had a decidedly childish sense of humour, often roaring with laughter, pointing at my sandals and asking where were my socks. My socks, as it happened, were all dirty and dancing around together in my laundry bag until I found a washing machine.

Later I had a long chat with this banker and one subject led to another and I told him that, somewhat to my surprise, I hadn't found the Germans xenophobic or racist in any way. Ah, that's because you are fair with blue eyes, he said. Germans like anyone who is fair with blue eyes but his wife back in Hamburg had Ukrainian dark looks and the Germans gave her grief all the time. They are very strange, the Germans, he added. Give them an idea and they'll all chase after it like sheep. But, basically, they hate everyone.

This banker was pretty strange himself *and* he was a German. He had inherited some large parcels of land in the old GDR, which he was sitting on, hoping the prices would improve in unification. The trouble was the old Communist Party bosses had now turned into 'capitalist bastards' and kept writing to him about his land. Once they wrote to tell him that his land had become overrun by rats and, when he came here to inspect it, he found they'd turned it into a car park. Recently they told him another piece of his land was slipping down a hill and that he must build a new wall to stop it slipping away altogether. 'I told them the land could slip as far as it wanted. I wasn't going to pay for any new wall.'

Well, I guess he must have known a lot more about the Germans than me but he really was a strange cove himself – unwilling to use the camp showers until he knew exactly the time when they were going to be cleaned so that he could then be first in. So I had to tell myself quite firmly that I always had to take people as I found them and not as other people found them.

I later took a quiet walk through the countryside around Colditz, still much enjoying the mellowness of the autumn as toffee-coloured cows, anchored in the fields with huge weights around their necks, bellowed their discontent, suddenly and ferociously, like caged lions. The sun was still in charge of blue skies and we were later to learn that this was the hottest September for 50 years. Lots of black squirrels were squirrelling around in the trees where little else moved except the odd sycamore seed as it helicoptered down through elegant shafts of light.

I was pleased to find that, at such moments, my mind had become alive with prayer again. Here, in this autumnal and inspirational landscape, and in the absence of anyone else, God had become a true companion. We were again having long chats with one another, often walking hand in hand in those falling leaves, as father and son, and I was feeling more spiritually content than for a long time.

On some days, as on that resurrection morning in Wittenberg, I felt – and still feel – that he was even physically opening doors for me, showing me scenes and introducing me to personalities which, at one time, had almost been crucial to his continuing work in his wonderful world.

Now, a long way from home and with my body still in an uncertain state following my operation, he was making me feel safe, just being here in this Colditz dusk, a cheerful companion and helpmate, who would always be around if I stumbled and fell. He could often act like the angry Old Testament father, flashing the cold edge of his disapproval but, at moments such as this, I felt I had won him around: that he might yet pay up next term so that I could go on the school trip abroad like all the rest of my mates.

CHAPTER 3

Caterpillar Devils

The sun was straight up out of bed on the dot the next morning as I escaped from that camp in Colditz – heh, heh – and continued surfing that golden autumnal wave down through Germany. The giant propellers of the new wind farms turned slowly in the warm breezes and the Saxony villages slumbered around stagnant, brown ponds where dragonflies hovered and ducks, their little feathered behinds poking up into the air, foraged for food. Even that early, heat hazes, suggesting the locality of a cooling oasis or two, were forming in the petrol fumes on the busy road.

I was still in the old GDR and they were still tearing up the roads with such a speed it was as if the whole country was about to run out of petrol next week. The truck stops were large and confusing with a fair sprinkling of female truckers who had the peculiar macho swagger of their male colleagues. I was having a cup of coffee and a bit of a think at one high counter when one of these women came and stood next to me, putting down a plate of food. She smiled at me brightly before taking chewing gum out of her mouth and putting it on the side of her plate whereupon she ate her food and, when she had finished, popped the chewing gum back into her mouth.

Back on the road again old defunct factories with smashed windows and redundant chimneys stood around in sad, unemployed groups. Weeds and shrubs grew out of their walls and abandoned machinery littered the vanquished yards. These places had clearly been found too inefficient for the new, unified Germany but I do wonder. The Tories closed all the coal mines back home in Wales for the same reasons and with disastrous social consequences. People need to work and I'd already met a few men who said they'd felt more happy and secure in the old GDR. Their working lives hadn't all been for nothing, they kept insisting. We may have been inefficient but at least we'd all been in work. We may not have been really rich but none of us had been really poor either. The Communists had always made sure we had *something*.

I was actually getting to enjoy driving these long distances because I was finding that this book was coming together in a rather strange but positive way. On some of my pilgrimages – as on the last one to Compostela in Spain – I had to dig quite hard for my material but what seemed to be happening on this one was that, as I drove, my mind was a bare stage when, every so often, an idea, insight or even a descriptive line staggered in from the wings, a bit like a drunk who had lost his script, and collapsed on his face in the spotlight. Then it just lay there, as dead and done in as a corpse when, maybe half an hour later, another drunk might do the same.

Sometimes they rolled up three at a time and, at the end of the day, with my pen in one hand and a glass of *vin* in the other, perhaps with Bruce Springsteen crooning to me on the cassette player, I would sit in my camper, pick up my notebook and wander along this line of corpses, turning them over or poking them about with my foot, wondering if there might be any life or promise in them and, if there might, whether I should revive them with the oxygen of a few words or even set them up in the larger intensive care unit of a paragraph, if only to examine their full figures and see how they might stand on a page. Then, in an equally strange way, they seemed to disappear from my mind altogether and, the next day at the wheel, a new line of drunks started to stagger into the spotlight only to fall flat on their faces and lay there as dead and done in as corpses, etc.

The trouble was there was now one drunken chimera which kept wandering onto the stage of my consciousness and refusing to die and be dealt with by a sentence or paragraph in my notebook like the rest of them. This image was of two hands holding up a sheet of paper to a church door and nailing it there to hammer-blows which were so loud they often made me jump. Those hands were flickering brightly in my mind at least once a day but why did they keep flaring up again and again? Why wouldn't they just disappear like the rest of them? What might those two hands be trying to say? Or was this yet another of God's little tricks? I might find out but, there again, I might not. You just never knew what was going to happen when he was around with you on The Road, as he clearly was on these sunny days in a German September.

The city of Erfurt, with her thick gathering of parish, collegiate and monastery churches, was once a real spiritual powerhouse where Luther first became a student and then decided to become a monk. Indeed, the city was even once called the 'Rome of Germany' and Luther himself called it a gold mine. 'There had to be a city here even if it was burned down straight away.'

Yet you could take the place as yet another of those old Communist fortresses as you drove into it, surrounded as it is by marching phalanxes of Stalinist apartment blocks even if each apartment was clearly nicely kept with huge red avalanches of forsythia and geraniums frothing over the balconies. Then there was what was left of the old wheezing light industry and the usual gaudy lines of advertisement hoardings. It was a real surprise, then, to come across the extraordinary city centre, full of wonky, disappearing streets connected by shadowy medieval alleyways.

Medieval houses crouched around flowing canals and many of the townsfolk were moving around on bicycles in the cobbled, pedestrianized squares. Every so often a tram went sliding past on metal tracks. Canals, bicycles and trams. What lovely constituents these are for any civilized city, each going about their business in the quiet murmurings of water, the whirring of sprockets and small clangs of bells. I sat outside a restaurant gazing around me and feeding my spirit with all this ancient modernity.

But again, as in Leipzig, there was a more profound silence in the air which I could not quite understand or define; something which made these old Communist haunts really special. Then I got it. There was no Radio One. I have wandered over almost all of Britain and even in the remotest parts almost every opening door lets loose a wailing shriek of Radio One. But that wasn't so here. I did pick up the pounding bass from the radio of the odd passing car but mostly it was a pleasant, soothing music of bicycles, trams and canals.

And just sitting there sipping a coffee I wondered if the new unified Germany was going to catch up with this place too and sweep everything that is so graceful away in a bedlam of speed and motorways and all that came with them. The answer could only be, yes, they would. And then open the door to all kinds of other 'horrors' while they were at it. Only the night before I had been talking to a traveller who told me that as many as two or three prostitutes were now working each of the lay-bys on the roads in 'new, free' Czechoslovakia. The Reds certainly wouldn't have put up with that and neither were they keen on drugs, although I came across one shop, just up the road here, Werner's Head Shop, which sold little but special Rizla rolling papers, bongs, fake skulls, hippy jewellery and books on how to grow your own cannabis.

Another strange neo-modern note was struck when I used one of those huge, mechanical public lavatories in the car park.

Every surface inside was stainless steel and, as the doors closed and I sat down, I half-expected the whole thing to take off to Mars. Piped harpsichord music was adding to this air of unreality when the music stopped abruptly and I looked about me, startled as a female voice began speaking to me in German. I don't know what she was saying – 'Have a nice day' or 'Hurry up down there' – but then the harpsichord began playing again. Soap, water and hot air came out of a series of concealed taps and Mrs Hal began addressing me again in her tinny, computerized voice. Then, as the doors opened and I stepped out she said: 'Auf Wiedersehen' and I half-turned and gave her a little farewell wave.

Later, as I was following a map on my way through a medieval labyrinth of lanes and shops to the Augustinerkloster, where Luther had lived as a novice and a monk, I came out into a small park by the side of the canal with a gathering of about 30 or 40 punks. Their clothes were torn and completely black. Their hair was red or green or both. Rings through their lips and noses added to their general air of belligerence as did some rather nasty Rottweilers who looked as if they would have been more than pleased to take a nice big lump out of you. Empty wine bottles and beer cans lay strewn around. I sidled up to a few of them in an attempt to make some bright conversation but got nowhere. They merely scowled at me and looked away.

I finally came to the huge central square with two large churches opposite me – the cathedral and St Severus' church – both close together, atop a hill and joined by a large series of steps flowing down between each of them like a huge stone waterfall. On the one side of the waterfall was a ruined stone pulpit where Luther had once addressed the crowds of Erfurt. Over a little further way again was the Bombay Curry House.

We can perhaps see the young Martin all too well, spread

out over those stone steps as a student, smiling cheerily at passers-by as he waited for a few friends like Spalatin and Jonas who were already calling him The Philosopher. There was a roar of life in him which young people always found attractive and, if there was a laughing group anywhere, he could usually be found in the middle of it. He could talk the head off a postage stamp and also liked to drink a little beer which the college authorities tolerated. He was also musical and learned to play the lute here.

But beneath all this merriment there was a deep anxiety because all his young ideas were being thrown against the high brick walls of cold logic, tricky dialectics and sequential logic. And, as they were flung, they were smashed to pieces. He was also being exposed to the discipline of Aristotelian argument for the first time which, if nothing else, taught you that you had to be careful what you said and how you said it.

So this student on these cathedral steps was in real turmoil; he was not learning anything so much as finding out what he didn't know; not understanding a lot either so much as finding out what he didn't understand at all. These were also the days when his lifelong struggle between reason and intuition would have been set up inside him. It took him a long time to accept that all you really need to be holy is a sense of fear and trembling.

And so, running amok in these lovely Erfurt streets, he took his Batchelor's and Master's degrees and was set to become a lawyer when God intervened. He was walking in the nearby village of Stotternheim when he was caught in a thunderstorm. There is a plaque there, on a granite block and in a grove of trees, marking the spot. 'Sacred soil. Catalysing point of the Reformation. In a lightning bolt from heaven Luther was shown the way on 2 July 1505.' The storm was so ferocious it engulfed him in a cloud of terror, making him call out: 'Help me St Anne and I will become a monk.'

Thus he set the path of his future life and he was soon saying goodbye to his friends and his law studies by joining that Augustine monastery over there in which he fully intended to shut himself off from the world forever. The cloisters are as they were then and, taking refuge in their coolness, on yet another hot day, you can sit on a stone bench and keep gazing into the middle distance until he comes past. And what would you ask him? To try and describe, perhaps, the enormous burdens of pain and fear which he must have been carrying when he first signed in here.

But to get even closer to his spirit walk around to the adjoining Augustinian chapel and, if there are no peaked caps about, try lying on the gravestone of Johannes Zacharias, face-down and with arms outstretched in a cruciform position. Kiss the hard gravestone and recall that Luther took his monastic vows in exactly this position 500 years earlier. Kiss the cold stone and imagine you are finally kissing goodbye to all your friends and carefree student days. Kiss the cold stone and say hello to all those long and lonely days of bitter defiance, fighting the Church, the Pope and the whole divinely sanctioned empire that was Rome. Think on all these things and feel a hard knot of fear as you kiss the stone that once kissed Luther.

He was later ordered to become a priest and ordained in the cathedral. And so it all finally began: this strange, intense journey to God, at first through books, vigils and prayers but then through profound soul-searching until he finally discovered that the real path to God lay through the heart, ordered by intuition and based on faith. In medieval times the heart was always seen as the key to the understanding.

He suffered much until he began uncovering such simple truths for himself. But suffering, generally, is what happens to you when you fall into the hands of professors in their academic citadels. They kill your faith with their well-honed lies and demands that everything be fully explained and defined. They butcher your young ideas and destroy your better instincts. Learning is not the way to God and, as a broad rule of thumb, the thicker you are, the easier the act of faith becomes. Get a formal modern education and it is only then with a little luck, and the grace of God, that your faith will ever recover. Martin learned all that the hard way and only ever came to God and a new self-confidence when he chose to let God grow in his own heart, trusting the dictates of his own conscience.

There was an unruly sense of mutiny abroad in the landscape later that afternoon with several fires burning distantly and sending up thick, ragged columns of black smoke. Small dust storms seemed to be moving around too although as I got closer to them, they turned out to be clouds of chaff and dust sent up by the combine harvesters. The dying sun caught in these dust clouds, bathing them in an unreal light and tidiness. In fact they reminded me of the Megiddo plains in Israel, where I had once stood at about this time, watching similar clouds of dust wandering through the sunset as the goat herds were being driven back to their pens for the night.

I found a campsite nearby and chatted briefly with a few lads from the South Wales valleys who had come over here to work on the roads. They were clearly putting away a fair bit of drink in the evenings, boasting that this was about the only campsite which would now put up with them. They had, it seemed, been expelled from almost all the other campsites for the usual Welsh crime of being drunk and disorderly. It is curious, I have often thought, that Wales was once the home of mighty temperance movements, that the valleys gave birth to socialism and the chapel and yet all most Welsh youngsters want to do with their money, after working so hard for it, is to get absolutely hammered with drink for as long and often as possible.

I cooked up a meal of pasta, sardines and Jalfrezi curry in my camper – largely because they were the first things I laid my hands on in my food cupboard – and later, with my belly rumbling continuously like the insides of a hot computer, I wandered out onto the edge of the campsite and watched the sun setting down a marvellous red crown on the surrounding hills and fields. A few ducks flew overhead. Again my mind crossed the world and I saw the sun going down behind Masada with shafts of red light slanting across the black, featureless depths of the Dead Sea and lighting up the high rock cliffs of the Hashemite Kingdom of Jordan.

The Holy Land entered my thoughts often and, on some days, pictures of the country settled in my mind with such force – and stayed there for so long – I felt a strong and urgent need to actually be there, almost as if the country had become my home which, after many visits there, perhaps it is.

The motives for any pilgrimage can be many, although you would have to say that fellowship was an important factor which was why I was now fetching up at more and more campsites rather than settling for the lonely isolation of such places as football car parks. I certainly had an unusual conversation that night with a former town planner from Brighton and a retired engineer from Cleethorpes on a subject which would certainly never have been broached in the presence of Chaucer's voracious notebook.

It turned out that the three of us had recently had heart by-pass operations and so there we were like three old ladies standing on the corner of a Welsh mining valley town discussing our recent ops. The retired engineer horrified me when he said that he had tried to lift up something really heavy like a car and one of the metal pins they use to stitch your breastplate back together had popped straight out of his chest. The town planner had to go back in and have his redone which was a real bore since they had to slice his chest open again, leaving it stiff and sore for another eighteen months. My chest was still sore and stiff all the time, I said, but, for the most part, it just tickled a lot. But the scar, which looked like a zipper on a pyjama case, did make me feel self-conscious, particularly on a French beach last year since everyone seemed to stare at it because the French, it seems, absolutely adore looking at any kind of wound. Oh, no one can see mine, said the town planner. It' s gone.

Their wives were absolutely appalled and went off for a walk together when we then started showing our operation scars to one another. The town planner's zipper had indeed gone although whatever remained was concealed by chest hair. You had to squint hard to see the town planner's too but mine, I showed them, still looked almost as fresh and bloody as the day they'd been stitched. It was all down to needlework, we decided. You see, your stitches almost look as though they've been embroidered professionally. But mine could well have been done in a frantic haste by Frankenstein's aunty.

The three of us really seemed to enjoy entering into what St Paul once called the fellowship of suffering in that chat and, of course, it also told something about the kind of people who were on The Road at that time of year. The kids had now long gone back to school and these two were clearly retired, restless souls, unwilling to rot and die in front of their televisions and still wanting to explore distant parts of the world, looking for those fleeting moments of truth. I kept bumping into them all the time on that trip, usually when I'd stopped looking for them.

Later there were crowds everywhere and the three of us were making our ways up a brightly lit street. Many were sitting on the pavements with huge slippers on their feet and showing clear irritation as we stepped over them, wanting to get closer to a river on which there was a procession. A large, ornate ship was the first to pass, followed by a couple of smaller ones. Then a loud roar went up as a man floated past dressed in a huge white and silver chasuble. His hair was long and he looked up at me with huge red eyes when I noticed that he was actually floating about a foot *under* the water.

I turned to the town planner and engineer but they couldn't make head nor tail of it either. The sound of hammering began breaking through the continuing roar of the crowds and a sheet of paper was being nailed to a door by a thick pair of hands. I cried out in terror, sitting bolt upright in my sleeping bag and staring around in the darkness of my camper with wide eyes and sweat pouring from every part of me.

Three words finally came to mind. Sardines. Jalfrezi. Pasta. Perhaps not the ideal combination – together with a few glasses of the town planner's feisty home-made wine – so I had better become a little more discriminating in what I put down my throat or it was going to be nightmares without end.

The next afternoon I was sitting glorying in the prettiness of the garden of the birthplace of Johann Sebastian Bach in the venomously charming town of Eisenach in Thuringia. The flowers had long lost their summer exuberance but there were still lots of golden rod and marigolds for the bees to sniff around. A few roses were still defiantly hanging on although I mostly enjoyed the way the sunlight actually seemed to have got right inside the vine leaves hanging around the windows.

All this and the music of the great composer himself since, directly behind me and in the house, which is now the Bach museum, a young man, Uwe Fischer, was playing various short pieces by Bach on a harpsichord, organ and clavichord to a small audience. Rock 'n' roll is my usual meat and drink but even a musical pygmy like me can easily appreciate Bach's huge range, from the simple melodies which chase one another around like a hamster in a wheel to the huge surges of worshipful passion in the organ. All Bach's music has an intense spirituality and I've often thought we can sense something of the complex personality of God in it.

Our restless, unsleeping God often wanders the earth seeking out people who mediate his spirit to his people, I believe. Bach surely became one such target and Luther another. Had these two men been contemporaries they would have been neighbours since Luther attended the parish school in Eisenach and was hidden away in the Wartburg Castle here when he was on the run from the Pope after being outlawed at the Diet of Worms. In fact Luther's fine house – now another Reformation museum – is in the next block, just around the corner, and you could all too well imagine both of these geniuses popping into one another's houses to borrow a cup of sugar or something. Or maybe Bach would have hurried around there with a new composition to ask Luther what he thought. Luther, never short of three opinions on anything, would say: 'Oh, it's fine Johannes. But, if you really want to know the truth, it's a bit too fiddly for me. Don't give up the day job.'

The one genuine surprise of my pilgrimage so far was that no one had really upset me, which had once been such a real fear for me. But nothing is forever since I then met a man in charge of that campsite who was forever rushing around with all the subtlety of a panzer attack and shouting at people, usually for not driving the right way around the obscure one way system around his office. This man could have shouted orders for Hitler and he had a real go at me for picking up a parking ticket and going on about how the *Polizei* would be after him if I didn't pay it. This was complete nonsense but he then went absolutely ballistic when, just to wind him up, I told him that the *Polizei* could chase me all they liked but I *still* had no intention of paying it.

But, far from being German, he was, in fact, from Manchester and, even worse than that, a fan of Manchester United so everything he said – or shouted – did not matter in the slightest.

Wartburg Castle, balanced high and perilously on an outcrop of red rock, looks as if it has just escaped from the pages of a children's fairy tale. But you don't actually meet any ferocious dragons as you flog your way up the steep, twisting footpath from the car park: just the usual array of attendants, frankfurter salesmen and itinerant musicians – all anxious to relieve you of your money.

It was a real climb too, made all the worse by the heat and the milling throngs of tourists going either way, all huffing and puffing up and down the path and smiling at one another with a weary sympathy which goes beyond language. You couldn't have got more out of the way if you were on the run from the law or the Pope, here high above the Thuringian forest, on the outskirts of Eisenach and almost completely surrounded by wooded hills. The kingdom of the birds, Luther called it.

Once over the drawbridge and into an oddly shaped courtyard it was difficult to fasten on to the atmosphere of the place because it was so crowded with long queues waiting to pay the hefty £4 entrance fee. They say they need to charge this for the upkeep of the castle but why the German government is spending billions repairing perfectly good roads and neglecting the upkeep of priceless cultural assets is beyond me. They had been having the same sort of struggle to keep going in the Bach House, Uwe Fischer had told me. They had lost most of their original musical instruments in the war and could now only replace them when they had any spare money, which wasn't often.

Inside the castle we were marched around in groups from one room to the next with the door always being locked behind us so there was no way of escaping from the group and going solo. I'm never much good in a group, particularly when there was one real idiot in it like that oaf eating a peach and letting huge gouts of juice dribble over the polished floors. And it turned out he was English too. But not from Manchester as I had at first guessed. Liverpool.

It was an odd castle; cold as most castles are but made even colder by the lack of furniture in the pillared rooms and frescoed great halls. The pillars and frescoes were certainly something else but you can't relax on a pillar or take a nap on a fresco. The few old chairs there were you couldn't sit on either and even the chapel looked a bit browbeaten and down-at-heel, devoid of any real ornament and with a few faded murals. Here they had put all their effort into the highly ostentatious great halls which told you something you didn't particularly want to think about. And much of the history of the place was lost on me anyway because the guide spoke almost exclusively in German, although when she discovered I was English – when I asked if I could escape the group which I couldn't – she did tell me a real story which managed to calm me down a little.

Legend has it that Luther was once so bothered by the Devil in this castle that he actually threw a bottle of ink at him. They even used to show pilgrims the ink stains on the wall. When these pilgrims began chipping away bits of the wall – because that is clearly what they like to do with old walls in this part of the world – the castle authorities said, oh well, let's try Plan B and just throw a fresh bottle of ink on the wall every year.

The trouble with Plan B was that the pilgrims kept chipping away at the wall, which was soon riddled with so many gaping holes like our Berlin Wall, that the authorities said, right, it's Plan C, which involved plastering over all the holes, painting the wall and pretending there had never been any ink on it in the first place.

I like such stories which seem so truthful while also telling us much about pilgrim stupidity and bureaucratic duplicity. Guidebooks and history should be lively and truthful although they are hardly ever that. They always become turgid and self-conscious and, as a travel writer, I think I can put my hand on my heart and swear I've never pinched a line from a guide book and pretended it was mine. As a broad rule of thumb, if it appears in a guide book, it ain't any good. Or it's a lie. Or nose-bleedingly boring.

A commercial television company in South Wales once asked me to write a short book about them. I began with everything that went wrong on their first night on our screens and followed that by all the exciting promises they had made – and failed to deliver – when angling for the franchise. They took one look at the first draft, said that's all very amusing and fired me on the spot.

I can't believe Luther was very happy in the ten months he was hidden away here although, perhaps predictably, he didn't take to his bed or the bottle but settled down to translate the Bible from its original text into German – as you do. I managed to spend a few quiet moments on my own in his old cell, admiring his desk and whalebone footstool while also thinking of this crusty old rebel dog, as cuddly as a sack of nails, who always called a shovel a shovel.

His popularity, I was coming to understand, rested on his wonderful ability to communicate with the common man and he was always thinking along these lines when he was working on his translation: 'We must ask the mother in the home, the children in the street, the common man in the market place about this, and look them in the mouth to see how they speak and afterwards do our translating.'

So the translation wasn't a cold, empty work of art like the castle in which it was conceived so much as a folk Bible for the common man who, Luther believed, used the same language as God. This Bible ushered in a new age of literacy and it also began a tradition which lead to the Tyndale Bible. John Tyndale also pledged that, thanks to his efforts, the boy who drives the plough would know more about the scriptures than the clergy. He used the language of the farm worker too, giving us such sayings as 'the salt of the earth', 'the signs of the times' and 'the powers that be'. So it was these works, then, which brought the Reformation to the people and ushered in a new age of literacy.

And so there was Brother Martinus, the object of my distant and continuing admiration, sitting there with his feet up on his whalebone footstool, laughing with a group of friends after they had done yet another long stint translating. They would all have some beer and a game of cards afterwards to relax, perhaps listen to music or make some of their own. Cards and music remain a part of the tradition in Lutheran homes after this great man taught us how to marry earthly pleasures with heavenly thoughts.

The six high towers of Worms cathedral needled a clear sky, set on a grey skyline of low-lying buildings and surrounded by vast, ironed acres of agricultural land. There is an incongruity about the cathedral which you also pick up as you approach Ely cathedral on the flat Fens of England. Both of them just sit there, brooding darkly and out of place; vast, elaborate ships of God which somehow lost their way home to a proper harbour in the city and ended up shipwrecked in the wrong place.

The closer you got to the cathedral, the more out of place she seemed to be. Violent daubs of graffiti smothered the walls of the railway bridge and there were the ubiquitous signs for McDonald's. Advertisements are clearly banned in most of the German countryside or on motorways but the twin, golden arches of McDonald's are forever to be seen on the side of carts placed in the fields, or on tractors or stray bales of hay or even peering coyly through a small gap in a forest wall.

We will never know if Luther would have appreciated a Big Mac with large fries but we do know he was ill with a high fever when he was summoned to appear before the Emperor at the Diet of Worms. He had already preached in

Erfurt, Gotha and Eisenach on his way here and the buzz had gone around everywhere about his defiant stand against the most powerful and complete empire since the days of Julius Caesar.

'Luther is coming!' the townsfolk kept saying, crowding these very lanes in their knee-length tunics and ankle-length skirts, the men in black caps and pointed shoes, the poor in clogs and rags, as ever. Their mood was belligerent too as they watched him make his way to the papal gallows. They were in the mood for a fight if they did try to string him up. 'Luther is coming!'

The word had long gone out on the street on how Luther had been excommunicated after he had publicly burned the papal bull in Wittenberg. Now they were going to take further draconian measures against this priestly pestilence. His arrival, in a two-wheeled carriage drawn by three horses, was heralded by a watchman's trumpet. He was dressed in a monk's cowl and accompanied by three friends. His safe conduct had been guaranteed but then revoked and he was extremely tense since not only was he low with a fever but he was convinced that Worms was a nest of devils. There were more devils in Worms than there were slates, he had declared and he was sure they were already roughing him up, not only by making him fall ill but by gathering his enemies all around and hoping to make him look a coward by making him run for it. It was ten o'clock on Tuesday, 16 April 1521.

The Devil was an ever-present reality in Luther's mind. He was convinced the Devil reigned supreme, often turning up in many forms from the foul sulphur taste in his beer to the crazed practices of the papacy. There were territorial devils and devil princes. The Devil was as big and wide as the world. Devils even lived in caterpillars and moved about in the same way. Now he was about to take on all the massed devils of Worms.

Just next to Worms cathedral is Heylshof, a small, delicately patterned park, alive with fountain music and the encircling traffic stuttering over the cobbles. Dead leaves crunched underfoot and a young girl with red hair was walking a dog. A squeal of childish laughter hung in the falling leaves together with the aggrieved clinking of an invisible bird, possibly a magpie. It was so hot – even for this time of year – my pen was slippery in my hand.

When the time to face his accusers had come Luther would have walked right by this bench on which I was sitting, passing that girl walking her dog and crossing over to that building there which was no longer a building so much as a scattering of ivy-clad ruins and a few shorn pillars. A small cell stands on one side with some relatively new mosaics of Christ and Luther in one of the old archways. 'Little monk, you are treading a difficult path,' a troop commander told him as he went inside.

About 20 of his books were on display when he was finally let in and John Eck asked him if he was the author of these books and if he would recant any of them. After taking a night to ponder on these questions Luther returned to the Diet and, by torchlight, because it was night, he summoned up all his confidence in the law of the heart and said: 'My conscience is captive to the word of God. Thus I cannot and will not recant, for going against my conscience is neither safe nor salutary. I can do no other. Here I stand. God help me.'

Everyone there knew the collision course had been set. He was not adding or subtracting a word of his fierce, sensational attacks on the Pope and council who had often got it wrong. Medieval superstition was no longer enough. The Christian conscience should be liberated from the chains of papal decree and canon law. A man only ever justified himself and his works by faith. It must have been a truly thrilling moment to have been there and seen history in the making in one man's mouth. *I can do no other. Here I stand.*

The cathedral bell rang over Heylshof: a strong, imperious sound speaking of the unmistakable authority and primacy of the Roman Catholic Church. Not that Luther was ever allowed to set foot in the cathedral after behaving as he did and, immediately after appearing before the Diet, he was taken back to his lodgings in Johanniterhof, in central Worms.

He wouldn't have much enjoyed the cathedral anyway, you guess. It certainly has the vast proportions of a cathedral but there is a certain shadowy bareness inside it, if not a sense of neglect. You had to pay to go in and there is a lot of the usual cathedral stuff, but I came across a stone Madonna with cracked lips, an extremely pockmarked St Christopher and an angel which had lost its nose. The chapels seemed excessively gloomy too and the extremely elaborate altar was a bit too elaborate for me; one of those ecclesiastical knickerbocker glories you also find in places like Santiago de Compostela in North Spain. The organ was also so high up the organist must have been a bit of a mountaineer, with ropes and an oxygen mask, to get up there. 'Destiny is like a cauliflower which grows equally in all directions,' someone called Carolyn had written in the Visitors' Book, which seemed to just about sum it all up. Or not.

When Luther finished his brief appearance at the Diet his friends and enemies made a tremendous racket as he emerged with his arms raised saying 'I am through.' His troubles were far from over, of course, but – even with all the devils encircling him – he may well have smiled as he made his way back to his lodgings had he known of all the memorials they would one day put up to him in Worms.

They built a Reformation memorial church on the other side of the town which is suitably austere. There is also a Luther's Gate and a highly polished Luther museum with a lot of peaked caps watching you closely in case you try to make off with any of the pictures, prints or an old Bible of his with an inscription in his tight, spidery hand. But easily the most elaborate of all these memorials is the Reformation Monument in Lutherplatz in which a group of bronze and stone figures portray the history of the Reformation. John Wycliffe is there, as are Peter Waldo, Jan Hus and the pugnacious Savonarola watching out for any sign of human vanity. Luther stands in the middle of them, gowned and clutching a large Bible, right shoulder thrust forward and head held high as if trying to avert his gaze from the ignominy of all the smiling Japanese tourists gathered around his feet and being snapped for the family album back home in Tokyo.

His original lodging house on the corner of Hardtgasse and Kammerstrasse has long gone and it is now a pedestrianized shopping centre with large department stores, bread and coffee shops and the inevitable McDonald's. A simple plaque marks the spot where he once stayed and, just a little further up the road, REM was singing on a loudspeaker, set up in the street to attract buyers into a bookshop. An odd pilgrim moment here, looking at a plaque recording the former presence of my favourite religious leader while listening to the painful brilliance of one of my favourite rock 'n' roll singers. What, I wonder, would Brother Martinus have made of Michael Stipe's singing? How could even the leader of the Reformation fail to have been moved by the pure and penetrating emotional truth of, say, *Everybody Hurts*?

Luther was virtually a prisoner in this lodging house for the ten days he was in Worms and he received a steady stream of visitors who were still urging him to modify his stand. But there were supporters too, some bringing him wine and others offering to take up arms if he felt his safety was threatened in any way.

But, in such a difficult situation, you need time to be alone and pray so he would have surely slipped out of the back door at night, roaming the streets, looking in through the lamp-lit windows and occasionally sending up prayers to God to give him strength in these fraught Gethsemane hours. Nevertheless, even as you walk behind him, you can feel the tension in him, the dryness in his mouth, his heartbeat actually quickening when he thought of what was to come. Courage is all very well but it surely can't be too much fun with that itchy, cold rope around your neck and then dangling from one of the Pope's gallows.

We walked down several streets together, coming out on the huge stone bridge over the Rhine, both leaning on the parapet as the lighters sped beneath our feet along the river. Over on the right bank was a young woodland of willow, ash and oak. On the left bank was a funfair with a giant Ferris wheel irradiating the night with whirling golden laser beams.

This was a holiday weekend for Worms so we went down the stone stairway in one of the bridge towers, pausing to take a beer in the tavern before broaching the gaudy merriment of the fair where the people were clearly enjoying themselves so avidly. It was exactly the tonic he needed at that moment. Joy and worry moved through his fat features as the young girls screamed out in delicious fear as the truly terrifying Space Rider turned them upside down and flung them around and around – and all at the same time. We moved on to look at the other big, fast rides such as The Magic House, Tombola, Space Shuttle and Ferris Wheel which even the fearless challenger of the authority of the Pope didn't want to get on.

The extraordinary range of the stalls sold everything from dog food to toy guns, bows and arrows, dolls' clothes, leather jackets and hats, pottery, bath oils, candles, handbags, sweets and wind chimes. Moths danced dementedly in the stalls' bright lights.

Food was being served up by the steaming ton – bratwurst, curry wurst, pommes frites, huge woks full of frying champignons, sausages fatter and longer than you ever dreamed possible. The big tents had wine and beer stalls with some twenty different wines on offer, sold either by the glass or the bottle. The Germans sank a fair bit too but there was no evidence of any violence or aggression in them – just a fundamentally decent people all out for a night of fun.

We had a few more beers in one of the tents and I told him

that perhaps a funfair like this should be his real memorial – not those dull, Reformation statues in the park or those potty museums with all their 'personal' memorabilia which may, or may not, be authentic. For his real legacy, surely, was that he taught that, while people should be God-fearing, they could enjoy themselves too. They were allowed and needed earthly pleasures, particularly to help them through times of oppression and loneliness.

And here people were doing just that: abandoning themselves into a screaming fellowship of fun on a warm night on the banks of the Rhine beneath a faint, crescent moon. This was his real gift to the people of the world: the simple ability to enjoy themselves.

When he finally left Worms Luther did preach again but his life was 'under ban and double ban'. The emperor passed an edict which said that you must not take him into your homes. 'Nor receive him in court, to give him neither food nor drink, not to hide him, to afford him no help, following, support, or encouragement, either clandestinely or publicly, through words or works. Where you can get him, seize him and overpower him, you should capture him and send him to us under the tightest security.'

The authorities also made a bonfire of the outlaw's writings so his life had become very hazardous indeed when a group of horsemen ambushed him and carried him off to safety in Wartburg Castle. The news of this ambush caused great excitement in Worms and soon Lutheranism began spreading even through the clergymen who began acting like human beings by taking a drink or two and actually getting married. And it wasn't too many years before Worms became two-thirds Protestant, a ratio it has maintained to this day.

CHAPTER 4

A Place called Dachau

I took the road south out of Worms, heading down towards Munich, with this bright autumn still showing no sign of moving into a black winter. If anything, it all might even have been turning back into the summer again since there was almost a new rhapsody of ripening fullness in the gardens. The tomatoes had become rich and red on dying stalks: the orchards were apple-heavy and wasps were zooming around looking to drill holes in those that had already fallen. So come and enjoy the warm embrace of my arms for a few more hours yet: say yes to the proffered gift of life as you watch the approaching slow train of death.

Such were the colours of my new mood of optimism which had begun to envelop my pilgrim soul in Germany, enjoying the wide variety of sights and sounds which were being constantly thrown up on The Road, happy and relaxed with God all around me, a true companion.

A small herd of deer had come down to the edge of the motorway, a few grazing on the grass verge but others looking up at the passing traffic with big, black eyes almost as if they were about to make one great, suicidal leap under my wheels at any moment. I stiffened and tightened my hold on the steering wheel. Deer were not particularly well known for their knowledge of the Highway Code and there had been frequent signs warning us to watch out for them which I had always assumed had just been put there for tourists.

So there they were for real and what was I going to do if they did decide to leap under *my* wheels? Brake? Try to avoid them? Run them down? I know what you were *supposed* to do, particularly on a busy motorway, but I wasn't at all sure that I could actually do it. Yet, as it turned out they didn't do anything at all except give the traffic big, black stares and, with a blow of relief, I accelerated on my way.

Even on these impersonal motorways there was still much to stop and admire. The colours of one field caught my eye and I climbed into it to find serried ranks of sunbathing roses, their flowers and fragrances still strong for the time of year. The Germans, I have found, adore flowers and are forever giving them to one another on almost every occasion from birthdays to simple visits to friends. Now and then I picked up the odd rancid smell of a piggery, always amused to look around and not spot a house anywhere. No one could live in a pong like that.

But the great glory of the morning was still those rustling forests with the winds throwing up eruptions of dead leaves on the roads until, at moments, I half-believed I might have been in some sort of triumphal procession with a ticker-tape welcome of brown and gold leaves fluttering down all around my camper.

A glorious morning, then, on which to sing harvest festival hymns. A shining morning in which every fault is hidden away in dark forests as the whole world puts up her ravishing face to a warming sun. There could be nothing remotely evil about such a morning, you would think, except that you would be dead wrong there since this sunshine road was actually taking me to the *Konzentrationslager* at Dachau.

I had no idea what to expect as I picked up the sign to Dachau Memorial Park since, had we been murdering Jews or religious leaders in Wales in the last war, we *might* have been prevailed on to leave the camp intact, but we would also, surely, also have tried to grow roses over it and pretend it wasn't there.

Not so in Dachau because – even so early in the morning – I pulled into a huge car park in which there were already seven parked caravans. KZ – GEDENKSTÄTTE. 9.00–17.00. Mondays closed. The car park attendant spoke good English, telling me the time the 'English' film was on in the cinema. I walked straight into the camp by crossing a railway line and passing a high watchtower. The old electrified fence was intact and a large blockhouse was on my left. The huge main square was about the size of ten football pitches and built around a central avenue of poplars. Far from being covered with roses there were no flowers or colours anywhere. Everything was a cold grey and, yes, there was no birdsong.

They had taken most of the old blockhouses down but had carefully reconstructed one with the old lavatories, mess halls and wooden bunks. Some 400 men would have once lived in these rooms originally designed for 50. Cutlery had to be kept spotlessly clean, a sign said. No mark or spot, however small, could be left on one of the tables or else a penalty was immediately forthcoming. If anyone tried to escape everyone had to attend the subsequent roll-call, having to spend a full night and half a day in the square, often in the cold and snow. 'Tolerance means weakness,' the Camp Code began with a jarring stylistic savagery. 'Beware of being caught lest you be grabbed by the neck and silenced by your own methods.'

Dachau was the first concentration camp and became a prototype for the others. Some 206,000 prisoners were incarcerated in here, of whom 31,591 perished. A former munitions factory, Dachau became the first training ground for murder for the SS while many were 'annihilated' by work and malnutrition. The inmates were mostly Communists, Jews and priests who were confined to the so-called *Priesterblock*. The Nazis treated the priests with a particular venom, forcing them to clear the snow in the winter, making them sing German love-songs, using them as medical guinea-pigs and putting them on a roll-call lasting for up to seven hours. Twenty died on one such roll-call as the camp leader preached 'funny' sermons to them. 'You dunderheads, you sluts, you motorized wild boars. Your Peter and Paul rock will be blown up but our rock will remain as hard as steel.'

Martin Niemoller, the Lutheran theologian, was also locked up in here after he began denouncing the pagan tendencies of Nazism and supporting the Confessing Church. A strong and picturesque personality, he turned down several offers of release as long as he renounced his religious convictions.

After wandering through the blockhouse I went into the museum where I came across a series of huge black and white photographs with blistering impact. They began with a machine gunner in his watchtower, then there was the suicide tangled in the barbed wire, the punishments of hanging from a tree by the wrists, the solitary confinements and beatings to death. They also conducted 'medical' experiments on some 1,200 prisoners which included infecting them with malaria. A flogging table with a whip was also on display as were descriptions of various stages of the 'final solution of the Jewish question'.

I was looking at some photographs of the Warsaw Ghetto and at one in particular of a terrified child with a floppy hat, holding up his hands with a Nazi holding a rifle standing behind him. I had seen this photograph before in another place and on another pilgrimage and my memory took me back to the Holy Land again and the Holocaust Memorial Museum in Jerusalem.

The museum had put on a special exhibition on the Warsaw Ghetto which was where I had seen this photograph before. Apart from the searing photographs they also had the exhibits of the ration books, the victims' shoes and spectacles, the threadbare clothes and the yellow stars – all the emblems of a special kind of evil and my belly had kept churning around as I looked at them. We had also seen the main Holocaust shrines in Jerusalem with their eternal flames but nothing had quite prepared me for when I went down into the adjoining Children's Memorial. You walk down a long underground ramp and through swing doors before stepping into a corridor of glittery darkness. Looking around and through a series of windows and mirrors you discover they have created the effect of surrounding you with a galaxy of thousands and thousands of stars. Each star represents the life and death of a child who died in these concentration camps. Doleful Israeli music is also played as a voice, on a tape-loop, continuously reading out the names of each child and the camp in which they had died.

It remains the most devastating memorial I have ever seen and our group had been unable to say a word for at least an hour after leaving it. I often think of those stars and the way I had come out with my eyes full of tears and my belly churning with a useless anger. And here it was all again, so to speak, that boy with the cap and eyes wide with terror, shuffling me along a distant corridor of memory to Israel before bringing me back, with the same feelings, to where it had all really begun, here in Germany, in places like Dachau.

The other visitors to Dachau that day were all silent too, I noticed, far more silent even than they might have been had they been inside a cathedral, as if they too could make no sense of it all and find the words which would somehow enable them to face up to all this. Even the thickest seemed to understand the redundancy of words when standing in front of this throne of evil. There really was nothing in the Scrabble bag of words to deal with any of this.

At 11.30 a lot of us filed into the surprisingly large theatre where, on wooden seats, we saw a film which sketched the history of the camp. It was set up by the Nazis, who called them protective custody camps, largely to deal with their political enemies. Books were being burned and Goebbels was concentrating on the 'Jewish question'. The inmates were soon being murdered and tortured, especially the Jews who were given the hardest and dirtiest work. When the camp was liberated on 29 April 1945, the Americans found, long before they even got to the camp, a freight train filled with corpses. In the camp itself they found 30,000 survivors of 31 nationalities.

'I wish everyone alive could come and see this,' Brett Harris of the USA wrote in the Visitors' Book.

I left the museum by the rear door, needing some fresh, clean air and walking the length of the camp compound on my own. There was no one in sight, just a slight breeze on the gravel which seemed to carry its own sorrow. Even in the broad daylight so many wounded ghosts were wandering around and I knew I wouldn't last a minute here at night. I headed for some distant church spires in a small pine woodland, hoping for some spiritual comfort there although the first building I came across there was the crematorium with its high chimney. Fresh flowers sat in the gaping holes of the ovens. Their iron doors were open and you could reach out and touch their coldness. They weren't always cold, of course, since these ovens once worked day and night. Corpses had to be piled up in the mortuary because there wasn't enough fuel to keep them going.

Just across the small yard were the gas chambers, disguised as shower rooms. You can walk through them. For some reason these particular gas chambers had never been used and those who were to be gassed – usually the Jews, the chronically sick or the insane – were transported to Hartheim Castle near Linz which had its own gas chambers.

I retreated into the small woodland nearby. Sun broke through the pines and I found a large wooden cross with the inscription For The Thousands Who Have Died. My already exceedingly fragile balance toppled over at that point and I crashed to my knees and asked God why? Why did you let it happen? Why didn't you do something about it? Many of these men were your private lieutenants and you just let them down. *The voice of your brother's blood is crying to me from the ground.*

You chose to show yourself on this earth in the shape of your son – *A Jew*! – the very embodiment of gentleness, radiance and joy. So what was this Old Testament nastiness all about? You could have surely stopped all this dead in its tracks but there are sides to you we are never going to understand, aren't there? Turning women to salt, flooding the world, levelling cities, destroying armies and then regretting it. Sometimes even you don't seem to understand yourself. How can we be expected to have any sort of love relationship with you when you don't even understand yourself?

We also had two world wars in which millions died and children were murdered in places like this. What was that all about? What happened to the so-called loving father and where were you hiding your face? You made the world, so you could surely have done something about all that. Haven't you heard the news that so many then turned against you, emptying your churches and giving up the faith because of all this?

I waited on my knees for a few answers to my angry questions but none came. A few birds did sing in the waiting silence. My nose sniffed a lot and a plane flew overhead. I turned and looked back into the wood where some sunshine suddenly brightened a shadowy clearing. But that was it. That cold indifference again.

Martin Luther taught us that faith is not something you can buy like a loaf of bread. It's something that takes root in your heart and grows out of tenacious search. Well, you grew in my heart for sure and the search has been long and tenacious.

So why, then, do you always insist in making it all so difficult? You kept setting Luther new challenges and, being the man he was, he responded to them. He didn't run away. But I would run away from you and all your complexities in a flash if I could. I would stamp you out of my heart if only I knew how. Except I don't.

The long and short of it is, on dark days like this, I get truly fed up with all this Christianity lark and yearn to carry on without you like most of my friends. Make a good living selling houses or insurance instead of writing these stupid books. Be happy without all the guilt. Be what I want to be and tell the truth only when I feel like telling the truth. Be honest only when there is something in it for me. And certainly be relieved of the problem of trying to explain to my sceptical friends where you were hiding when those Nazis were butchering people here in Dachau; how you stood back and let all these broken bodies drown in an ocean of suffering.

My anger with God did not abate – and might even have got worse – when I then went to have a look around a group of small churches and memorials which had been put at the end of the camp. In fact one of them – the Church of Reconciliation – made from reinforced concrete, simply had the effect of making me feel very ratty indeed. It had been the architect's belief, it said on a leaflet I found there, that everything in the original Dachau camp had been made out of right-angled things – the camp itself, the inspection place, the flogging table and the foundations. The architect therefore decided to design this church with no right angles at all – only curves. Ah so.

There is one right angle in the courtyard which reminds us of a rifle range not far away in Hebertshausen, the leaflet said, where the SS murdered thousands of Soviet prisoners of war. They should not be forgotten.

The church should also largely be built underground, the

architect decided, because depth is not only a symbol of suffering and death 'but also of contradiction and resistance'. It's also a symbol of shame, he went on, as if you wished the ground would swallow you up.

Some may be able to detect some sense in all this nonsense but I can't. But the real surprise of such daft, architectural conceits, I have often thought, is not that architects have them but that they then carry on to raise small mountains of perfectly good money to realize them.

I examined the other buildings there distantly and with little curiosity since I now had the hump with everything. They included a Carmelite convent where the sisters had an active prayer life based on reconciliation; a pretty Russian Orthodox chapel with an onion dome and walls made from tree trunks and an impressive chapel of atonement, put together from rough stones and looking like a gigantic wine press topped by a giant crown of thorns.

I'd had enough of all this by now and walked back down through the avenue of rustling poplars, pausing for a moment with a few leaves drifting all around me when my riven and ragged feelings picked up on the edges of God's sorrow. Another moment of complete hopelessness then when it was as if he was crying too, trying to calm down my churning anger with the balm of his everlasting grief.

In a message which was both coherent and incoherent he seemed to be trying to tell me something of his powerlessness in controlling such evil when men actually choose to embrace it. I wasn't in the mood for any of these slippery evasions but he kept *insisting* that it was the case. Man is either free to do what he wants or he becomes imprisoned within the dictates of my holy will. *And there is nothing at all that I can do about it because that is how I made him.*

I tried to brush him away and step around him but he wasn't having any of it. *I didn't make man a robot but a person with a free choice*. I tried to pass him again but he was obdurate. *Man can't have it both ways and neither can I.*

This is an old stance of his. Pick a fight with him and he will occasionally creep away and sulk. But sometimes he comes fighting back. You're never quite sure how he will fight you but fight you he will – either with fiery visions or his tears or in your dreams or through the mouths of other people or even – *bang, bang, bang* – with the image of a pair of hands and a hammer, nailing paper to a church door. *Bang, bang, bang.*

After the turbulences of Dachau I gathered up my bad mood and headed down through the lush meadows, Dracula castles and cuckoo-clock villages of South West Bavaria. Soon I found myself on the so-called Romantic Road, a name of impeccable daftness, probably another of those tourist board confections which, in itself, means nothing. The road was rising high into the Bavarian Alps and the air outside was becoming quite chilly, mirroring how I was feeling inside. Light showers of rain fell on my windscreen.

Everything was happening so fast I couldn't take it all in. I needed some quiet time to rest up and heal; to recover the balance which was so often the object of my prayer life. Maybe I could find something to help me in Steingaden, a tiny Bavarian town which also had the Wies, the most famous pilgrim church in Germany.

Even in the rain the mere sight of the white church, just sitting in a lush, green meadow against the magnificent backdrop of the Trauchgau Mountains, lifted my bruised spirits a couple of points. The building really did have a milky majesty about it and even though hundreds of pilgrims were thronging the road, since this was clearly a special day, I was also quite astounded by the bravura glory of her interior with huge coloured frescoes rolling over the ceiling in a breaking wave of light blues and golds. Angels and apostles rode clouds. A cross floated in the heart of a sun and the figure of Christ was enthroned by a brilliant rainbow. All around were white pillars topped by gilt leaves and vines while the high altar was a positive riot of rich ornamentation. Even the pulpit was the most wonderfully worked I have yet seen, looking like a gondola bursting out of an unfortunate smash in a Christmas bazaar. Yet, it has to be said that, despite all this richness, the place has an abundant freshness and radiance. They had not only been working with gilt and paint in here; someone had been giving a lot of thought to light and there was nothing faintly oppressive here. You could also tell, from almost any vantage point you cared to take up, that every single inch of this church had been burnished with the deepest tender loving care.

The pilgrimage here began in 1730 when two monks carved a figure of Christ for the Easter procession. Contemporary fashion frowned on the baleful look the monks had given the figure so it was duly consigned to an attic, later becoming an object of devotion by a farmer's wife. A few weeks later tears began falling from the figure's eyes as she was saying her night prayers before it with her husband. A small wooden chapel was built here, saying six Masses a day and attracting pilgrims from all over the world. Soon designs were drawn up for this new church which was consecrated in 1749 and is now believed to be so important it is also a UNESCO Cultural Heritage of Mankind Building.

The original wooden sculpture of the weeping Christ now stands at the centre of the altar. His long, battered body is heavily chained and its simplicity stands out attractively against the ornamental sumptuousness all around. The shrine itself is crowned by a golden pelican: another symbol of Christ's death on the cross since it was believed the pelican tore open her breast to feed her young.

I sat for maybe an hour on the pews taking all this in with the aid of a guide book but, strange to report, this church, perhaps the most perfect, if not the most beautiful, church I have ever been inside, did nothing for my troubled spirits. I could see and appreciate all her undoubted qualities with my eyes but my heart remained distant and untouched. My long morning in Dachau was clearly still glooping through my system and, to be perfectly honest, I'm sure I would have been far better off and certainly happier sitting drowning my sorrows in some dingy pub.

There was no chance that, on this day of all days, I was going to settle any of my differences with God and even less chance that, in my present mood, I was going to go down on my knees and worship him. We were emphatically no longer going out together and I was still seething with dark and angry accusations, still stiff with pain like that poor chained Christ up there. No wonder he cried so much when he had a father like his.

The long and short of it was I was so browned off with him I was considering giving up this pilgrimage altogether and going straight home to my wife who, at least, never gave me a hard time like this. But, if I did pack it up here, that might well lead to a lively quarrel about the publishing ethics of advances paid and work not delivered. A quarrel which I was also not likely to win. But perhaps I could come back here next spring and take up where I left off? That plan had always been a possibility anyway if the weather turned against me. I didn't know anything at all, having wandered straight up a dark cul-de-sac and finding no way out. Oh, what to do?

What I did know was that I didn't want to stay in this church any longer and, when one of the stewards gave me a worship sheet because a service was about to start, I just waved it around uselessly for a moment before putting it down on the pew and leaving.

I was also extremely tired so I drove about three miles down through rain mists to the edge of a lake and, just as darkness fell, curled up in my sleeping bag right there. The rain began drumming heavily on the roof of my camper but I was too exhausted to be bothered by that – or even any strange dreams – only waking up a few times to pull some more clothes over me since the mountain air that night might even have been a few degrees below zero.

I slept for around twelve hours that rainy, cold night in Bavaria and awoke, rubbing my eyes and blinking into one of the most glorious Sunday mornings I have ever beheld. Cow bells rang dully in the fields and whole avalanches of warm sunshine were crashing down the sides of the high, pine-studded mountains. Wide strips had been cleared in the forests, perhaps in preparation for the skiers and winter snow and two single puffs of clouds were crossing the clear, blue skies above the mountains as if two Red Indians on neighbouring peaks were having a quiet morning chat. All this romping sunshine also glazed the surface of the empty lake with just a lone man rowing distantly through this great, burnished mirror evidently on the trail of a few unwary fish.

The air was as fresh to the taste as lollipops and I turned and turned again on the axis of this savage magnificence, feeling the closeness of God again with him nudging me in the side and saying: *Look. We all know what those Nazis got up to but see what I can lay on for your breakfast and I'm not even trying. Just look at all this*. So I held out my arms, raised my smiling face to the sun, closed my eyes and, seeing the peculiar golden blaze in my brain when you do that, said: 'Oh well, let's put it all behind us, shall we, and see if we can actually manage to enjoy this pilgrimage together.'

As it was a Sunday I thought I'd go back to Steingaden for the morning service only to find that a good half of Bavaria must have had the same idea since the church meadow was a sea of parked cars.

Ah well, I'd press on, slipping the Three Tenors onto my CD player as I drove slowly up into the Bavarian Alps. A fine morning, to be sure, the sun high in a clear sky, those dramatic mountains looking down at me and Pavarotti singing his socks off. I was travelling extremely slowly too when I noticed that I was being followed by a mile-long procession of cars. But none of them seemed to mind: not one of them was swinging out to see if they could get past me, all of us enjoying this fiery, worshipping morning in heaven.

It was on that long, slow road to Oberammergau that I knew that I had got right inside this pilgrimage; that I had become really involved in it and that it was ultimately bound to take me that little bit closer to the heart of God.

You really can't buy faith in a shop, as Luther kept telling us. It's a long, hard road, often through ice and darkness. And as we tiptoe over the ice and pick our way through the darkness we learn, often through painful experience, how we can become better and more faithful. The onus is always on the pilgrim to enter into an intelligent and creative relationship with God when he is on The Road. The pilgrim should be prepared to accept the downs when, as often as not, God will hold out his hand and help him with an unexpected up.

Such is the Path of the Cross and no other path in this whole wide world matters. *Bang, bang, bang*. There it was again.

CHAPTER 5

A Passionate Village

The tiny Bavarian village of Oberammergau might just have wandered out of the pages of a Grimms' fairy tale with neatly cut piles of wood piled up in the gardens of the wooden cuckoo-clock houses. The clear, pebbled River Ammer curved through the outlying meadows and goats wandered up to visitors on the river banks hoping to be fed. The surrounding mountains gazed down on the village in the stony, majestic way that mountains do and, in fact, the whole setting was so comically picturesque you half expected Julie Andrews and all her singing brats to come dancing down the slopes at any moment.

Church bells rang out over the house rooftops and flowers spilled out of the balconies. Many of the walls had highly coloured frescoes or air paintings which tricked the eye although a large smelly cowshed in the town centre provided a slightly jarring note. Inside a row of cows had their tails tied up to a rafter and just outside the door was a pile of smelly cow dung, parts of it fresh and faintly steaming, bringing much pleasure to the attendant flies.

Even if you spoke to no one at all here and just moved around looking you could work out a lot. There was nothing poor or peasant-like about this place, you noticed immediately from the long rows of gleaming, high-performance cars parked around the squares. The church was also well looked after and almost every grave in the church cemetery had fresh flowers on it. The swimming pool was also one of the most modern I have seen with saunas, a wave machine and a section which comes out of the side of the mountain before turning back in again enabling you to swim out into the cold air in warm water, look around the valley and swim back in again.

This is also a village which lives in the shadow of the Cross since there is a huge wooden one atop one of the mountains which looks serenely down on everything. Lightning struck it in 1807 and it burned for ten days.

The shops were mostly not ordinary either but piled high with devotional carvings and religious icons. We are not talking Lourdes or Knock rubbish here either since many of the carvings, of such as Christmas cribs, dolls' houses and clock-cases, were decently artistic if expensive. Then, even more intriguingly, you notice many of the men, as they go about their business, have long hair and rumpled black beards, as if they had all just missed the last bus to Katmandhu.

This village, in fact, is the setting for the Passion Play, the most famous religious play in the world, which recounts Christ's last week on earth. Some 2,000 villagers are involved in its production and they were all busy in the 18-month rehearsals for the Millennium play when I rolled up there. Audiences of around 5,000 pay around £180 each for a two-night package and there are 75 performances in each season which, in any language, adds up to an awful lot of *sauerkraut*. Oberammergau is the richest village in Bavaria.

All actors are paid a percentage of the profits to make up for any loss of wages during the performance and the director receives around £10,000. Many manage to work around their appearances like, say, Werner Richter, a local taxi driver. He also drove the school bus, operated the ski lift and ran a guest house. As Esdras, a servant of Annas, the high priest, Werner only had to be sure to be there just for the first half an hour of the afternoon session.

The old theatre used to look like a collision between a huge covered railway station and a Greek temple. The audience sat in the railway station and the actors generally froze as they moved around the pillars of the Greek temple since Oberammergau is pretty much freezing cold all the year round, even in the middle of summer.

When the actors rehearsed they did so in ski caps and leg warmers so it did not help their blood flow either that, when the play opened, they mostly had to wear togas. Back in 1980 it actually began snowing on 17 June, during the Last Supper, much to the delight of the audience and the despair of the cast. Rudi Zwink, a former Jesus, said he was up on the cross for half an hour and his feet were blue when they took him down. 'I am not joking. They were blue.'

They were, however, putting the finishing touches to a new theatre on my visit, having put in new wooden seats, poured in new concrete floors and splashed out with a completely new roof which covers everything and will presumably mean that they will not be losing any actor with frostbite the next time around. No one challenged me so I had quite an interesting poke around backstage too, noticing the costumes and funny wooden swords together with the way the actors only had a tiny bit of a bench on which to change. They use almost a thousand costumes and have pens and cages for the animals and birds.

The animals have caused a few problems for the production over the years, particularly after one of the local farmer's horses was such an abject failure when he had his chance of stardom. The horse's problem was that he was scared stiff of bees and was wont to make a fast exit, stage left, whenever a bee zoomed past. He also had the unfortunate habit of urinating over the stage at moments of high drama, so he duly got the elbow and they had to import a better-trained horse from nearby Austria.

The local donkey has never been known to misbehave when he carried Jesus on his triumphal entry into Jerusalem though the local pigeons, who were standing in as doves, often fluffed their lines on release during the cleansing of the temple. They were supposed to fly straight back to their coops to be returned for the next performance but the problem was that, particularly if it was raining, they often took shelter on the ledge above the proscenium arch. There, as often as not, they sat around burbling to one another all day, messing up key lines and fouling the ledge so much the actors often had to get out a ladder and go up there to clean it up and encourage them to get on home.

The play was first staged in 1634 as a village thanksgiving to God for safe delivery from the plague. At the time thousands of people, even including doctors, were dying with a sudden and terrible swiftness. It was a time of mass graves and inter-tribal wars. A host of those Lutheran devils were walking abroad and even mad dogs attacked the people who were themselves often so hungry they couldn't put up any resistance to the plague germs. Here in Oberammergau the villagers gathered and swore before the altar that, should they be spared, they would perform a Passion Play. From that moment no one else in the village died and, with a few breaks for a few wars, the play has been performed every ten years ever since.

This play of the people also managed the unusual feat, for the time, of bringing together Catholics and Protestants. Matthew Arnold in 1871 said it brought together people who seemed 'as far as the poles apart', something it continues to manage to this day. This is the bare, unadorned story of Christ's last days before all the many churches got at it and put their own spin on it.

But it has also produced real dramas of its own as when, back in 1922, an irate spectator really got into the spirit of things and actually tried to shoot Judas. They have also thrown him into the river more than once and being attacked by angry women with umbrellas is accepted as one of the hazards of the betrayal business out this way. 'Someone has to do it,' a local plumber and former Judas, Martin Kratz, told me.

Hitler himself came to the village in 1934 and praised the play. 'It convincingly portrayed the menace of Judaism,' he said worryingly, perhaps proving that anyone really can read anything into any text. 'Pontius Pilate was a Roman so racially and intellectually superior that he stands out like a firm, clear rock.' Some later claimed the play made Christ into an Aryan hero but, in fact, it was less anti-Semitic than the Nazis wanted and they kept asking for a new text.

A number of changes have been made in the text over the years – largely to deal with any suggestion of anti-Semitism – and it is now presented as a theatre for the people in which the emphasis is on the way *everyone* was complicit in Christ's suffering.

Each of the 18 main speaking parts has two actors who alternate performances and can stand in for one another when necessary. All the actors must have lived in the village for the last twenty years and the play begins at nine in the morning and continues with a three-hour break for lunch until half past five. It is seen by the villagers not so much as a performance as an act of worship and the only make-up they use is for Christ's blood.

But even with two actors for the main roles it doesn't always go to plan since, in 1980, Rudi Zwink – or Jesus 1 – had a sore throat and got in touch with Max Jablonka – Jesus 2 – to help out only to find that Max had a terrible cold. Almost everyone had colds in that production and they all spoke their lines in between sneezes with wodges of Kleenex stuffed up the sleeves of their togas.

Max Jablonka ran a souvenir shop in the village and used to get really fed up with the price of all this fame. 'How can I sell my souvenirs when people come in asking for my autograph all the time? I have a business to run. Shops like this do not go on their own.'

Another similarly hard-hit was the barber. All actors, except those playing Roman soldiers, must refrain from cutting their hair or beards in the run-up to the new production, which was why a lot of the men in the street look like cosmic cowboys hoping to get to Katmandhu before the hashish crop fails. 'This play is a dagger in my trade,' the barber moaned, flinging his fat hands into the air. 'The visitors are only here for a short time so they are no good for business. Everyone forgets the barber. Would *you* like a haircut?'

One of the Roman soldiers recalled when he was in it and the director had them popping Jesus 2 up and down on the cross after he died. 'He made us do it four times and Max is no feather. Then we kept handing him to the Virgin Mary feet first and the director kept shouting it should be head first. There were only four of us too. The part was too much for four people. My wife kept complaining I was exhausted all the time.'

Another director was Hans Maier, a woodcarver by trade. Some of the cast said he was too tough on the children who had been noticeably reluctant to turn up to rehearsals on time. Others said he worked them too hard but all he said, in his defence, was that he had a definite idea what he wanted. He managed to squeeze 850 on stage when the crowds called on Pontius Pilate to crucify Jesus, he told me with the ends of his mouth curling with pride. And on some nights, abed with his wife and the dog snoring in front of the log fire, he dreamed many a lively crowd scene and he got some really good ideas from his dreams. His most difficult role was casting the play with the committee since there was intense competition for every part. He got a bit cagey when I asked him for detail. 'I can't tell you much but one of the Pontius Pilates only made it by one vote.'

I tracked down two of the Pontius Pilates, George Glass and Toni Preisinger, who were close friends and hoteliers. When they were not selling Christ down the river and then washing their hands of it they were always helping one another out with their businesses. They sent guests to one another if they were full or even the odd bottle of Scotch if the bar ran dry. Like almost all pilgrims everywhere, those who go to Oberammergau also drink like fishes. 'It's those Benedictine monks that are the worst.'

George Glass, with thinning hair and a cold look suggesting he could sell anyone down the river, worked his way up through the ranks from 1950 when, as a child of 8, he was in a crowd scene. In 1960 he got to be a Roman soldier. He later became a priest and then Pilate. He did try for Jesus but didn't make it. 'I didn't have enough hair for Jesus,' he added with a wry smile. 'And there were a few other reasons too. No, I'm not telling you what they were.'

I also met a former Virgin Mary, Theresa Fellner, who had brown-green eyes, a delicate, vulnerable face and the smallest hands. She was a student of 'social pedagogics' at the time and spent most of her time thinking about her boyfriend or worrying about her British Leyland car which, she said, was falling to bits and being eaten by rust. 'Trouble is, I just can't afford another one.' Often she drove around the mountains mouthing her lines and sometimes people spotted her talking to herself, clearly deciding she had gone potty. She captured this plum role after being Adam's child in 1970 and Mary Magdalene in 1980.

Local custom decrees that all the 150 female roles in the play should be taken by unmarried women, so a lot of young girls postpone their marriages until the play has finished. Indeed, when the 1980 season ended there were 20 weddings in the village in one week. Local custom no longer decrees that the women should be virgins, however. 'We would prefer it, you understand,' the director said, picking his words with the greatest care. 'But these are modern times so it is not – ah, what you say? – it is not a requirement.'

Jesus can get married if he wants to and some have been. The only social requirement for playing Jesus is that he is a decent sort of chap. Those who played the main roles often, in an odd sort of pension plan, end up in the chorus.

A play with so much ambition, which also generates a huge amount of money, does attract high levels of cynicism but the villagers don't really deserve it. There are the odd, greedy ones – the types who have anyway generally colonized the world – but when they say they genuinely want to portray the passion, death and resurrection of Jesus, in the spirit of a vow made by their forefathers in 1633, I believe them unreservedly.

The village was friendly and clean and I was invariably greeted everywhere with a pleasant smile – except at the barber's. The cast also had a great sense of humour, particularly one of the Judases. He had his neck in a brace and explained that he had spotted a pretty girl and jerked his head around so fast he had done his neck in.

It is a village I would love to have grown up in myself, if only because – it has long occurred to me – any aspiring young writer who grew up here would have a mammoth *Under Milk Wood* to write with such marvellous, universal themes it would undoubtedly travel the world. Any young writer trying to think of a subject to start his literary career should just go and live here and get to know everyone. There are the major religious themes connected with the play, of course, but, behind all them, is the larger and even more familiar story of what it means to be a human being. A story about a village like this is the story of everywhere. We all come from somewhere like this.

The only faint problem I encountered for that time of year was the multitude of wasps who were clearly wanting to stock up before the winter snows. In fact when I sat down for a meal on the outside terrace of one of the fine restaurants there it was a toss-up who was going to get my food first. No sooner had the plate been put in front of me than they came zooming in from all angles, not even much perturbed as I tried to swat them away with my knife and fork. When I later shook some sugar into my coffee I shook three wasps into it – 'Do you want one wasp or two?' – and they then proceeded to drown in it before being helped to the side with a teaspoon.

One man there had a serviette draped over his beer and, when they kept getting into it anyway, he began piling plates and cutlery on top of it. The couple on the next table seemed to come up with the best solution: the man actually poured out a huge hill of sugar on the end of his table which managed to distract most of them while he got on with his liver and onions.

This amiable couple turned out to be Robert and Jane Curry, both 77 and Methodists from Philadelphia in the US of A. They were clearly only too happy to come here too since this was their seventh visit, the fourth as a couple. The money from the play had done no end of good for the village and the children, Robert, a retired minister, said. As far as he was concerned the place was a little lump of heaven, which is as good an endorsement as it gets.

An evening hobble down a lane outside Innsbruck glorying in the warm moonlight and slight breezes shaking loose a few more autumnal leaves which crackled underfoot. They fell in ones and twos, some spiralling down fast and others drifting one way and another slowly. A horse nickered in the nearby darkness and over on the other side of that small woodland were the lights of that great Austrian city. Something small and furry dashed across the crackling path in front of me.

I was now halfway on my pilgrimage to Rome and

attempting to frame a huge web of prayer in my mind, something suitable for this night of moonlight on the mountains. I wanted to talk to him about where we had been and where we were going. This prayer was going to be a moment of tenderness and reconciliation: a time of forgiveness and love as I tried to understand the last two or three days and explain how it might be possible to come and trust one another more and not get into pointless quarrels which just upset everyone.

I was even trying to shape the air with my outstretched hands as I thought on all this when something caught my eye which was of the night and yet not of the night. It was a flash of light, to be precise, but not someone's torchlight: a bright, hard flash of light which twinkled with a diamond-like ferocity. Then it disappeared. I took two steps forward and stopped, staring carefully at the point where the light had appeared. There was something strange yet familiar about that light which suggested it might even have been the light of a passing angel.

Many people do not believe in angels but I have believed in them all my life and they have sometimes rescued me from all kinds of trouble. At one difficult time when I had a coal business – in a way which is far too complicated to explain – one of them even told me that my partner was stealing from the business. And that rescuing angel had appeared in much the same ferocious light as this one now.

Except that this one had now disappeared into the moonlight itself and I was still standing there awaiting its return. Angels represent the very arm of God in this world; they are constantly active with messages or rescue missions and will all appear in full force, the Bible tells us, with the whole army of angels mobilized, on the plains of Armageddon, just prior to the return of the Son of Man.

I remember driving across those very plains in Israel late one night and wondering if the time was at hand because I spotted quite a few blueish lights dotted here and there like giant glow worms. Well, I might even have been driving through the greatest breaking story of the last two thousand years, I thought briefly, until a closer inspection of those lights revealed that they in fact came from the television sets of the Bedouins who ran them off heavy-duty lorry batteries in their tents. Oh, how hard and fast our great religious dreams often fall.

I walked on to the spot where I had seen that light, gazing carefully into the woodland before looking back over the fields and up at the outlying mountains. Nothing moved and it was as if the very land had been becalmed in a huge sea of placid moonlight. Even the trees seemed to be holding their breath and the breezes disappeared.

Yet I remained quite calm, recalling the original purpose of my walk which was to frame a huge web of prayer within which we would come to trust one another. But I was sweating a little. And my heart was banging a bit too. Instead of prayer my thoughts were now turning to a soothing bottle of wine.

My calm then turned into a spasm of fear when I heard some laughter: not ordinary human laughter but distant alien laughter; the knowing sardonic chuckle of a Mekon perhaps; a carolling cackle of glee in the moonlight. I did not know whether to carry on or run away and, not knowing this, I just sort of dangled there, a freshly caught fish wriggling on the hook of his own fear.

A man stepped out of the woodland and stood on the path about fifty yards away from me. I couldn't make out anything of his features except that he was short and wearing some sort of long tunic. A few leaves fell around him when I heard that laugh again. With my blood running cold I took in a huge gulp of air and began running straight back to my camper, locking the doors from the inside, drawing all the curtains and reaching down into my cupboard until my trembling hand grabbed hold of the neck of a nice bottle of strong, red wine.

My prayer life hadn't yet got me where I wanted to be. That much was clear.

They don't exactly keep a welcome in the Austrian hillsides since you are required to pay a daily road tax on the border. Ah, I said, I'm only passing through very fast so I'll just take one day's worth. No you won't, they said. You've got to take a minimum of ten days' worth which was around £12. No way out or around it either. One woman tried to get out of it and ended up in prison. Now I wouldn't have minded a short stay in prison since I could have probably squeezed a lively chapter out of it but, as Austria wasn't really on my pilgrimage route, I paid up with a grump.

They're a funny lot are the Austrians: a bit like the Swiss who, when I passed through them later in my journey, made me pay a whole year's road tax just to go through the nightmare of their endless tunnels. What's the matter with these people?

But the Austrian scam turned out to be even worse than it had first looked since I had only driven no more than 20 miles from Innsbruck when I was back on another motorway where, despite my ten days' road tax – and my little green sticker on my windscreen proving I'd paid it – I had to pay again. This bit of motorway didn't last for more than a few miles either since it then brought me to the Italian border where – surprise, surprise – another toll gate was awaiting me.

Some lovely moments though, meandering through the Italian Alps with the sunshine falling down one side of the valley and rolling up the other in a interchanging scrum of light and shadow. The sun arrived late on the valley floor and left early. Every time you looked up at the sky it seemed to be moving around into a new position which could best show off the features of this great room, like the glazed lakes or the clouds wandering around distant peaks. These small hill towns were clearly gearing up for the snow with the ski lifts stretched right across the valley floor, silent and motionless just for now. Dorothy Wordsworth actually screamed the first time she saw the Alps.

Johann Wolfgang Goethe came this way in 1786 and began a fashionable pilgrimage in his *Italian Journey*, which is still followed by Germans to this day, as it moves out of Northern Germany and proceeds southwards looking for the light of the Italian Renaissance. 'From Bolzano to Trento one travels for nine miles through a country which grows ever more fertile,' he wrote. 'Everything which, higher up in the mountains, must struggle to grow, flourishes here in vigour and health, the sun is bright and hot, and one can believe again in a God.'

From time to time I stopped to just look but there was too much really: the houses, orchards and lakes, all coming together to make this great mountain panorama of changing light. Walkers were up and about on the stone paths, a strange tribe, if there ever was one, walking around and around in vast circles like goldfish in bowls. They always look so damned cheerful too. Why can't they be miserable like everyone else?

Small electricity stations stood on river banks and there was a marble quarry. I might even have found the point where Goethe began believing in a God since the bottom of the gorge evened out slightly and we entered narrow lines of vineyards with bundles of grapes hiding in the leaves. A few groups of workers were out with their tractors, clearly about to bring in the first of the wine harvest. Some great wines around this way too – Bardolino, Valpolicella and Montepulciano. I may not have been here before but I'd sure picked up a hangover or two from this area over the years.

Two huge fires were burning near one another high on the left-hand slope, their flames a milky yellow orange and the black smoke curling up into the sky. Well, perhaps as a Celt I had been here before, on another pilgrimage altogether, riding down here astride my horse, together with the rest of the boys, doing a spot of pillaging and looting as we made our way along the valley on our way to sack Rome. We often set light to something too, if only to let the locals know we'd been around.

We had done this journey a few times now, riding down from Northern Europe and on our way to rough up the Romans. It was a pretty awe-inspiring sight, even though I say so myself, seeing us picking our way along that ravine, our bodies covered with green woad, a skull or two dangling on our saddles, flask of wine in one hand and the reins in the other. Much has been written about why we kept attacking these southern regions but one of the main reasons was that we loved the wine down there and had developed quite an addiction to it. In fact most of the Celts' love of alcohol first came from this road leading down to Rome. We never knew how to make it but the Romans were terrific vintners so we went there, sacked the place and, when we'd drunk our fill, took the rest of their wine back home with us. The Romans got mad as hell about this and it was only to protect their wine that they started to arm and defend themselves properly.

We Celts loved fighting and worshipping strange, cruel gods before we were christianized by such as David and Patrick. Our idea of nirvana was to die in a massive fight with the bodies of our enemies piled up all around us. Anyway our souls did not die but passed on to someone else after our death. The only thing we really feared was that the sky would fall in on us. Otherwise we were always up for the cup.

But all that was more than a millennium ago and things have changed a bit, I thought as I tried to get my credit card to go into a machine which would then allow me to travel on the next stretch of Italian motorway. I like using credit cards on my journeys since it means I never really know what I'm paying out – since I never look – and I then take it all in one big hit of pain when the monthly statement arrives back home.

Yet I had never actually used my credit card in one of these automatic machines on motorways and, in consequence, I had probably shoved it into the wrong hole since the card had gone in but was now refusing to come out again. I went into the office to appeal for help only to be faced by about six Italians who clearly not only didn't give a damn about my credit card but cared even less about the huge queue which was building up behind my camper. More appeals followed and a few did finally consent to come and look at my problem whereupon they took out their car keys and had a good dig around the tip of my card which was still showing. This pantomime went on for about half an hour, with a three-mile queue stretching way back up the Italian Alps, when someone found the proper key and unlocked the back of the machine and gave me back my credit card which, it seems, I had put in upside down.

Welcome to Italy.

CHAPTER 6

A Shrine to Love

I was sitting on a high veranda directly overlooking Verona, as a blood-red sun sank down into a fluffy bed of grey cloud. The sky was alive with skittering bats and swooping swallows, all out frantically looking for a late supper, a swallow occasionally harassing a bat who quickly moved out of the way. The swallows looked to be better and stronger fliers than the bats.

The sun sank directly into that bed of cloud and, way out on the horizon, the airport lights were the first to come on in a long, twinkling necklace. Just then all the birds seemed to clear the skies, save for one or two stragglers, leaving just the distant virulent hum of several thousand motor car engines feeding into one another. The bark of a dog mingled with a man's shouts. A spired basilica sat serenely and alone on the prow of a headland to my right.

The street lamps began coming on in criss-crossing yellow lines, all spreading out into a huge buttercup meadow with just a few white lights, as bright as diamonds, scattered here and there. But even with the darkness being held up by this spangled maze you could still make out the crooked medieval postures of all the old buildings and churches huddled together inside the city walls; still make out the shining backbone of the River Adige as she curved beneath those arched stone bridges thronged by people out taking the night air, laughing and chatting together in groups.

A sudden and unexpected peal of bells rang out which was not so much a melodic peal as a series of hesitant, assonant thumps, almost as if they were being played for the first time or even tuned. This odd medley went on for about five minutes before another set of bells in another church repeated the same dull, uncertain refrains. You could see this bell tolling in the belfry since it kept letting out odd shafts of a light from below as it swung back and forth. The night was warm and soft; the air itself had the faint taste of toffee.

I was in the grounds of a castle directly behind the Teatro Roma in one of the loveliest campsites I have yet come across. Rows of tents had been pitched beneath vines on the battlements. There were also secret alleyways through the heavily wooded gardens where the autumn didn't seem quite so advanced as it had been back in Germany. The actual layout of the gardens was almost impossible to work out and my camper was almost completely covered by shrubs. I even had my own flight of stone stairs down to a washroom with flagstone floors and squirty taps which often didn't squirt anything at all.

The oddest people kept turning up here too, including a few street mime artists, a 63-year-old hippy from Paris and a young wannabe Israeli film director who was cycling to London. I asked him if he ate all the time he was on The Road to keep up his energy levels. Oddly not, he replied. When he was cycling he ate almost nothing but, when he took a rest day, he just ate all the time.

The elderly couple who ran the campsite were most unusual too: the man devoted to the different trees he had planted throughout the gardens and the woman who, refreshingly, didn't seem to care when – or if – she was paid. Local council officials often called wondering why they didn't do something more upmarket with this amazing location but they were happy enough offering food and a place to sleep to the poor pilgrims of this world, they said.

The only possible black mark against the place were the medieval lavatories which could even have been sat on by the great Galileo himself. They were but holes in the ground and came decorated by the thickest cobwebs made by the fattest spiders. Loo rolls were held aloft on bits of string and impossible to reach. So it really was Auf Wiedersehen to the all-singing, all-dancing lavatories of Germany. Not that I minded. I had enjoyed a lot of what Germany had to offer but was already feeling at home in Italy, especially sitting on this magnificent veranda and looking out on this city as her populace surrendered to the pleasures of this warm, toffee night.

In many ways the contrasts between Italy and Germany were quite dramatic and the atmosphere of my pilgrimage had changed almost completely. The Germans were fast, disciplined drivers who only ever moved into the outside lane to overtake. Many Italians seemed to believe they should get into the outside, fast lane and hold it no matter what. The concept of pedestrian crossings also seems to mean nothing to Italians while their most precious driving asset is their horn which they beep almost incessantly, particularly if they sense you might be in some way lost or confused. I showed a moment's hesitation in the middle of one of Verona's crossroads while looking for a sign and they surrounded me like a pack of hunting jackals – old men and young girls – all beeping away at me and gesturing for me to go one way or another as I sat there glowering at them, unwilling to be bullied. Happily I usually had a slight advantage in these confrontations since my camper was far bigger than any of their little, tinny Fiat Unos or those stupid mopeds which they insinuated into the slightest space in the traffic. Also few Italians wore crash helmets, even those on mopeds on which, even more worryingly, mothers often carried babies or young children.

The Italian approach to parking tickets was also extremely relaxed as I saw for myself that night in Verona when not one but four traffic wardens came down the pavement. Far from wearing natty uniforms designed to fill the erring motorist with terror they were all wearing shorts and filthy vests, chatting cheerfully to one another and handing out parking tickets to all and sundry which, I discovered on close examination of the one under my windscreen wiper, demanded the immediate payment of a fine of less than one pound.

But perhaps the greatest difference between the two countries was the money and the way you had to hand out thousands and thousands of lira in Italy. Even the smallest transaction seemed to be a bit like playing Monopoly so that when you paid for a few groceries, say, you took out a huge wad of notes and began thinking along the lines of 'Well, all right, I'll take Park Lane off you but you've got to take Marylebone Station and Edgware Road.' And you kept handing this woman more and more wads of money with her counting it and shaking her head, accompanied by a lot of sighs, until she finally nods and tells you that, yes, she will let you have Park Lane and she will take Marylebone Station and Edgware Road and that you can now get out of gaol.

Verona, with her narrow medieval streets and salmon-pink houses, was an easy city to get to grips with. Most of the old buildings and churches, together with the amphitheatre, were huddled within a few miles of one another in a small curve of the river. Every corner has a nice, crumbling feel to it and there were any number of faded frescoes and spalling patches of plasterwork. Most of the walls were also but beds for untold growths of weeds or shrubs with so many earthquake cracks on so many walls they would give any self-respecting house surveyor an immediate nervous breakdown.

The amphitheatre, empty today, once hummed with people enjoying all kinds of barbarities from gladiatorial fights to the hunting of wild animals and later jousting between knights.

Nowadays it's mostly used for opera: a form which is totally lost on me. I would find it marginally more entertaining having all my teeth out than having to sit through an opera. The stories are always rubbish and why do they always take half an hour to die? And *what* are they always singing about when they do so?

But the old churches of Verona were as fine a place for quiet prayer as any wandering pilgrim could hope for, even if they seemed oddly deserted, if not actually neglected. I discovered a nice detail in the Church of Sant'z Anastasia – a large stone hunchback near the main door looking truly fed up because he had a holy water stoup on his shoulders. Another was performing a similar feat on the other side looking either fast asleep or drunk. A real man with glasses like small, cloudy portholes did wander up to me as I sat in front of the altar, stared into my face so closely I was all but gassed by his garlic breath, then took off quickly, clearly thinking I was someone else. Probably an opera singer on his day off.

Yet there was nothing remotely deserted about one small courtyard there and the reason why so many of the churches were deserted, I guessed, was because everyone had come to Verona to see one thing and one thing only: this courtyard which contained Juliet's balcony where she called out for her beloved Romeo. Hundreds were packed in here as firmly as all those sardines in a tin and several of the walls were but a mass of tightly scrawled graffiti, usually crude paintings of hearts or the names of boys or girls. Even as I sat on a doorstep watching the proceedings a few more youngsters aerosolled their lustrous names on the walls. And all this despite pleas, in five languages, not to write on them.

Just next to the front door of Juliet's house was a metal statue of her completely painted in black except for her left bosom which had been polished into a bright gold by the many groping hands of all the boys who had been photographed grabbing hold of it. Smiling couples also stood in front of the statue to be immortalized forever in the family archives. A man took a woman by the hand and serenaded her with a fine tenor voice. Everyone clapped him when he had finished his little aria. Tired babies grizzled in their mothers' arms and there were more than a few in wheelchairs too.

A real madness hung in that courtyard air which was being brought to the boil by a series of people who were forever coming out onto Juliet's balcony just above the door, waving to the crowds below and again being photographed by their loved ones. A young lad with pink hair and a pin in his lips came out to wave at the mob; then came a pretty young girl in a Spice Girls T-shirt, a smiling Japanese girl busy videoing everyone below, an old lady who clearly should have known better and – we don't want to be too cruel about all this – oh, why not? – an enormous American girl who seemed to be built out of balloons and had a face so flat and ugly it looked as if she had just been French kissing one of those German dumper trucks.

Entry into Juliet's house cost L.6,000 which first brings you to a shop where, for L.10,000 I purchased a small book, *Shakespeare and Verona*. You can also buy sweets 'I baci' with 'speciality kisses of Juliet' as well as Juliet's liqueur for L.25,000 which 'recalls at any moment the charme (*sic*) of Verona'. You may also listen to an audio-tape about the house on a machine on the wall for L.500 or, for a further L.500 send a letter to Juliet, presumably to complain about some jerk who was breaking your heart, which you then put in a post box in the shop. I couldn't find out what happened to these letters to Juliet since the assistant wouldn't tell me.

You then climb the stairs – there is also a lift for wheelchairs – and wander around largely empty rooms with almost nothing to look at, or do, unless you yourself want to walk out onto the balcony and wave down at the crowds below. But I couldn't take any more of this imbecility and wandered off looking for a reviving drink.

In a way I suppose this shrine to love might well be the story of pilgrimage in a modern world which has completely lost sight of God. Where once pilgrims travelled hundreds of miles, often by foot, to venerate a holy man, they now often travel thousands of miles, often by coach or aeroplane, all searching for the illusion of romantic love which, at a guess, has probably been responsible for more grief and family breakdown than all our wars put together.

Where also they would once rub their hands over a holy object like, say, the statue of St James in the porch of the cathedral of Compostela, they now come to fondle the left bosom of a young woman's statue in Verona. Where they would once at least see a fortune in jewels or holy relics in, say, the shrine of Thomas à Becket in Canterbury, they now pay up to walk in empty rooms or buy pointless objects like sweets in the shape of Juliet' s kisses, whatever that shape might be. You also wondered if any of those in wheelchairs were there looking for a miracle cure as they do in Lourdes.

Even the book *Shakespeare in Verona* turned out to be total rubbish with a threadbare storyline heavily padded out with extracts from Shakespeare's play. Yet the ultimate irony of this deeply tacky 'shrine to love' must be that it rests completely on a work of fiction, and not only is it possible that Shakespeare didn't even know where Verona was, it is certain he never once set foot in it. They have even 'manufactured' Romeo's House nearby and Juliet's Tomb, an extremely suspicious stone sarcophagus which could even have once been a horse drinking trough.

Everything to do with this shrine was a fraud – presumably propped up by the Italian tourist industry – and, if nothing else, proved that, when it came to idiotic gullibility, we have not advanced one jot since medieval times.

The next day I picked my way out of the back streets of Verona and took the road to Padua which was not so much a road as a spaghetti of broken tracks making their ways through light industrial estates, small vineyards, fallow fields and past the odd hotel or restaurant. Dark foothills rose to my left dotted with the odd manor house or castle.

But here again I felt oddly at home in the landscape even though I had never been here before, because almost everywhere you looked you could see how effectively Italian culture had penetrated our own. The Soave and Valpolicella vineyards were nearby. Most of the small towns sounded like the surnames of Mafia hit men and almost all the restaurants looked like the same Italian 'greasy spoons' in which we have all eaten and drunk too much in British cities over the years.

Just before Vicenza I picked up a sign to Monte Berico, a well-known pilgrimage centre in North Italy, and turned up there to find, as luck would have it, a pilgrimage in progress. Charabancs and cars were packed cheek-by-jowl around the huge basilica as it squatted on the top of the hill overlooking the city of Vicenza which, this fine morning, was quietly smouldering beneath a dark cloud of diesel fumes.

The traffic up here was pretty thick too, with a few *carabinieri* trying but failing to whistle a bit of order into the chaos. I did manage to squeeze the nose of my camper into a field whereupon, as was my practice, I legged it as fast as I could before anyone could tell me to move it. This is one of the first rules of any motorized pilgrimage: park and then put as much distance between yourself and your vehicle as possible. The second is to have a vehicle so big and clumsy like mine it is all but impossible to tow it away. The third is to have foreign number plates since it is unlikely they'll chase you around the world to pick up the fine. (I say 'unlikely' since I did meet an Englishman later in Rome who had jumped out of America without paying a speeding fine and they tracked him all the way back to England where this £30 fine duly escalated to something like £800 and, this time, there was nowhere to run.)

The inside of the Basilica in Monte Berico was jam-packed with the choir singing beautifully and the congregation joining in enthusiastically in the responses. It was a High Mass with three or four bishops, in full regalia, moving about doing bishop things together with any number of romping children and grizzling babies. This was possibly a Marian Feast Day when everyone troops up the hill from Vicenza to show their devotion to Mary. Afterwards, there would be a big party.

What I have always enjoyed about being in Catholic services is the catholic nature of the congregations. Our own churches and chapels often have tiny congregations consisting of little more than a few old women with imitation fruit in their hats but, in this Basilica, the range was right across the human board – the mothers and fathers holding babies or children, the grannies in black bringing up the rear or grandads in ill-fitting suits and nicotine-stained fingers clearly worrying about when they are going to get their next drink.

You could also tell the emblems of faith were strong around here from the building itself, especially in the massed arrays of fresh flowers on the altar and the carefully polished ornaments; in the impressive care that had gone into the restoration of some of the old paintings and the cleanliness of the floors and windows which didn't even look dirty when the sun was shining directly on them. There was even a new Chapel of Restoration down below, amok with new fittings and any number of crestfallen penitents all lining up to confess any number of sins.

So on pilgrim days like this you can pick up on an enduring poetry in both the people and the manner and place of their worship which goes some way, I think, in helping you to understand how the Catholic Church has managed to hold and succour so many from one generation to the next.

As the Mass continued, many were lining up to go around

the back of the altar where they placed their hand on the stone face of the Madonna. When I'm in such places I also like to attach myself to any queue, in the same blind way as they do outside Russian shops in food shortages, if only to see where it was leading and what was going to happen. And here, today, I enjoyed that moment when I touched that stone face which had also been touched by so many over the years. Such points become places of mass communion: an energy point where all our pilgrim hopes are recharged.

The rest of the Basilica was slightly bewildering – an odd collection of antique guns with broken breeches in a glass case in the cloisters. There was also a shop and any number of big, rather formal paintings including one by Paolo Veronese whose The Supper took a lot of looking at and, in the end, was strangely and mutinously overwhelming.

At one point I stopped to watch a priest in a wooden stall performing a blessing on a large family gathered around him. The young mother, in particular, was following his words with care, only occasionally stopping to lightly cuff one of her children so that he'd pay attention. The father, holding a sleeping baby, seemed only slightly interested in the proceedings when, at the end of the blessing, the priest began showering the lot of them with gouts of holy water whereupon the baby woke up and began screaming his eyes out. But the mother was clearly well pleased with it all and told her husband to see to the priest with a nice big wedge of lira.

The foundation of this Basilica was tied to two apparitions of the Blessed Virgin which took place on this hill, it said in my guide book. The first was on 7 March 1426 and the second on 1 August 1428. But the guide book didn't then go on to say anything particularly interesting about these apparitions or who had seen them, just burbling on for another twenty pages or so about architectural features or the names of the worthies who had helped out with this or that.

I left Monte Berico, the smell of incense lingering in my nose and my belly full of pasta from the restaurant there, again picking up the road to Padua which turned out to be an odd, jumble of a city, flung down around various piazzas and with lots of shadowy, high buildings in the centre. I cruised these forlorn streets aimlessly looking for a place to park only to pick up a sign for the Basilica of Il Santo which brought me down to a huge statue-sentinelled square with odd lines of stalls selling votive candles and giant rosaries. And big though this square was there still wasn't a place to park in it until I found one in a nearby back street.

The Basilica of Il Santo, with its roof of grey onion domes and pointed steeples, looked like something which had just missed the next train to Istanbul, although I first went into the church of Santa Giustina, a towering brick building which seemed to echo to its own posturing emptiness and polished spaces. Anything that might have been interesting was clearly behind a locked door although, somewhat to my surprise, I came across a transept which contained no less than the body of St Luke, transported here from Constantinople. The tomb was inlaid with alabaster panels and I spent some time gazing at it and wondering what Luke might have had to say for himself as he may well have met Jesus and once travelled with Paul. Luke wrote the Third Gospel and the Acts of the Apostles and his writings form at least a quarter of the New Testament. Indeed, his gospel is often called 'the most beautiful book in the world', charting Christ's story and the fulfilment of prophecy through to his passion, resurrection and final enthronement.

But there was some doubt that his body was actually inside that tomb – a doubt underlined by an English notice on a nearby board. Scientific investigations have been conducted on the skeleton, it said, and so far they had come up with nothing that had contradicted the possibility that it was St Luke. Full results would be announced soon.

They had some relics of St Matthew here too, they said, and I found it all a bit worrying, particularly when I next broached the nearby Basilica of Il Santo – a truly remarkable swirl of every architectural style you have ever read about in every guide book – and found myself in the Chapel of Relics with lots of medieval reliquaries on display within glass cases. They had a casket with the bones of St Anthony in it and his tongue and chin in a head-shaped reliquary. There were also photographs of those who had been cured by the saint's miraculous intervention.

St Anthony clearly had a wide range of gifts and has ended up becoming the patron saint of miners and lovers, of the poor and women giving birth. A man once borrowed his psalter without permission and only returned it after seeing a frightful apparition. In the light of all this St Anthony also became the patron saint of lost property.

I've never been sure what to make of such holy relics particularly as so many are evidently phoney, often having been 'discovered' by monks wanting to beef up a flagging pilgrim trade. 'Pigges bones', Chaucer called them. But I guess they're harmless enough if that's what people want to look at or if they *feel* it can actually help them. A good cure is so often a matter of belief, my medical friends have often told me. Feelings of well-being are 90 per cent of the battle against illness.

Certainly Luther had some fun at the expense of these so-called relics when he drew up a list of such things as a good piece of Moses' left arm; three flames from the burning bush at Sinai; two feathers and one egg from the Holy Ghost; one long hair from the beard of Beelzebub; a half a wing from the angel Gabriel; a big chunk of the shout with which the children brought down the walls of Jericho; five bright chords from David's harp and the three lovely locks of Absolom's hair.

But you do want to ask a lot of hard questions and, in the absence of any proper answers, there does come a point when even pilgrimages reach a state of overload. With my mind spinning with relics, saints and miracle cures, I returned to my camper in that side street and decided to stay put right there, drawing my curtains and heating up a curry before settling down with a glass of *vin* and an inspection of the day's literal and metaphorical corpses for my notebook.

It was lateish and dark when there were three loud knocks on the side of my camper which all but made me jump out of my skin. In fact had I not been calm after several glasses of *vin* that's what might well have happened. It may have been the police, who you always half expect to come knocking when you're camping wild, but on peering out through a crack in my curtains I could see nothing moving anywhere in the side street except the cold and the darkness.

That might have been the figure of a man standing in a splash of lamplight out on the main street but I wasn't sure. In ordinary circumstances I may just have ensured I was locked in properly – or even driven off to find another side street – but for some reason I got out of my camper, which I locked behind me, before walking down to the main street to try and find out what was going on.

A lorry drove past with its headlamps picking up nothing but my own shadow, dividing it up and whirling it all around. Music was coming from one of the houses and I could see the ghostly image of a television set in one of the windows. I was undecided what to do, finally making my way around the side of the Basilica of Il Santo and coming out onto the huge oval square where, with a thumping heart, I looked at the many statues, holding my breath as if half expecting one of them to come to life at any moment. The night was faintly star-smattered and I kept on thinking of that laughing figure in the Innsbruck moonlight, wondering if he had come to visit me again.

No pedestrians were abroad but there was enough passing traffic for me to feel safe so, calmer now, I walked the length of the cobbled square, past all the statues until I came down to a canal. Other, larger, statues on horseback were standing around maintaining menacing silhouettes but again nothing moved or sounded louder than my beating heart. I may have caught sight of that figure again standing about 50 yards away on the edge of another puddle of light but, even as I stood there, he crossed through that puddle and seemed to disappear as if by a trick of smoke 'n' mirrors.

I drew back into the darkness and stayed quite still while another man – clearly drunk – staggered across the square without one good leg under him. An elderly lady with a hideously painted face which caught in the lamplight went rattling past on an elderly bicycle. A few more lorries chased one another around the square.

I wasn't likely to get much sleep in this state and, satisfied that my Innsbruck angel wasn't around any more, I wandered the square again looking up at the stars. It must have been somewhere near here that Galileo had first set up his telescope in 1609 before taking a good look at the night sky. He saw stars that no one had dreamed existed: whole constellations of distant glitter together with all the valleys and craters on a moon which had generally been thought of as almost pebble-smooth. He even spotted planets which moved and later wrote: 'I render infinite thanks to God for being so kind as to make me alone the first observer of marvels kept hidden in obscurity for previous centuries.' These discoveries changed his life although, perhaps predictably, they also set him on a collision course with the Pope.

There was an uncrowned glory about this evening for sure and I sat on a bench squinting up at the stars trying to connect with Galileo's hot and cold emotions as his probing lens fell on this and that *and this*. If you look carefully at a night of stars you will always find one which is especially glittery and you can take as your own.

The star has always been the logo of Epiphany, which marks the end of the season of Christmas; the star which shines through the darkness and trauma of our fallen world; the star which, as it once did for the Magi, guides us home.

Among the ancients the sky at night was the great world book; the stars were the letters and the constellations the words and sentences. As the stars moved so did the book's narrative change and move forward. Others believe the stars are the great book of God and, as we read this book at night, we should be able to feel something of his immensity, his wonder and his glittering perfection. We should be able, imaginatively, to even enter into his grand purpose. Stars are the tallow candles of the Celtic soul. They are the ancient lights which will guide you to the arms of the Lamb where all your suffering will end, all your questions be answered and your mission in this world made clear.

And so it was, in that starry Paduan night, that one Celt sat reading the great book of God by the light of all the tallow candles of his soul. The story was one of effortless and unimaginable brilliance; it told of a hurtling dash, packed with theatrical drama and mysterious incident, towards a surprising and even earthshaking end when there wouldn't be a dry eye in the house.

With this end the astonished and moved audience will rise as one in rapturous applause. Except that we haven't quite got to the end yet; not here in Padua anyway; not now just near Galileo's former home. Here for the moment we have a short interval in an empty square full of silent statues and a faint burst of alien laughter fluttering on the very edge of the night.

CHAPTER 7

The Miracle of Venice

As a jobbing writer from Wales for around 20 years now – after 15 years in journalism – the tide has always come in and out of my life and career. But this tide does not do so as regularly and predictably as that of the seas' since it can sometimes stay out for as long as a year but can then come in, for no reason, and, just as fast, go out for another two. Even when you are doing well as a writer, the general feeling is always of progressively going straight down the pan.

My finances have always moved erratically through three levels – broke, dead broke and bankrupt – and I've always thought I'd call my autobiography *Debt in the Afternoon*. My accountant actually breaks into uncontrolled laughter when I walk into his office each year while whole hills of alarms must go off in the tax office when they receive my tax returns. Twice now I have been invited to go in there and explain how I live on what I say I live on and twice I have told them about the wonderful advantages of my secret arts council in the shape of a working wife. All this seems to depress them no end since they are there to ferret out fraudulent claims but they have never found anything fraudulent about mine. You should forget about writers, I tell the tax people. Just cross them off your list.

Even monks on vows of poverty earn more than me and, all in all, I would have been far better off if I'd become a one-legged trishaw driver in downtown Djakarta. And the really bizarre thing about all this is that I am a *relatively* successful writer. The annual returns from our libraries have often had me in the top quarter of the most borrowed writers in the country. My novels have all sold well and been paperbacked. I've also won a few national awards so what other writers live on I just can't imagine. Not that I am complaining about our wonderful libraries. They send me a nice little cheque every January which just about pays the gas bill although I still dream about that fine January morning when I will receive enough to pay the electricity bill as well.

Yet for the last five years I've been on a new track, so to speak, forsaking the novel and becoming a professional pilgrim, spending months wandering across largely medieval landscapes while also trying to come to terms with my relationship with God and then write books about it all. Well, *someone* has to do it.

It's often not as much fun as it might sound – three days with no food and nothing on my feet in Lough Derg! – and, if there's little money in being a novelist, there's even less in being a professional pilgrim since you have to pay your own expenses out of your advance. At least the novelist gets to keep all his as he sits down all day looking at a winking cursor.

But having got those moans out of the way, I must own up to some truly great moments on the pilgrim road. That thrilling causeway over to Lindisfarne always lifted my spirits whenever I walked it. Then there were the lonely Skelligs off the coast of Ireland, a jagged fist of rock in wild waves where the Celts first shaped their unique character and faith. The first sight of the spire of Canterbury Cathedral after a long journey on foot from Winchester still stands vividly in the long corridor of my memory as does that ravishing dawn on the summit of Croagh Patrick mountain after climbing up there through a night of storms. My mind can still savour practically every colour in all those lurid, liquefying sunsets in Northern Spain on the road to Compostela.

In all those pilgrim moments, usually near sea or up a mountain, I have felt close to the heart of God, often feeling his undiluted pleasure and pride in the marvellous balance and great beauty of his creation. You can even, in such moments, feel tremors of his excitement as he shows you these scenes and says, well, yes, mankind may well be going to the dogs but just take a *look* at all this. And have a dekko at that. See the way light settles on those waves and have you ever seen colours as striking as those?

You know then that the pilgrimage is always for something, even if you are never quite sure exactly what it is at the time or when you have actually discovered it. Pilgrimage is an adventure into – and an exploration of – the very mind and heart of God himself.

On The Road you also begin to understand your relationship with him and we had again been getting on well lately in Northern Italy after a few Dachau hiccups in Germany. There again, this often happens on the pilgrim road when you manage to get away from the hourly crucifixions of your very soul and spirit by the media. Closeness to God is also helped by the presence of inspirational beauty as all those Renaissance church-builders and painters in Italy understood all too well. His spirit lives in such churches and, if you brood inside one of them for an hour or two, you can often hear him calling out to you although he may well then go on to tell you something you do not want to hear.

Such was the general drift of my thoughts as I sat on a jetty in Fusina, warming my face in the morning sun and waiting for a water bus to take me across a huge lagoon to Venice. It was a truly wonderful morning – a *buongiorno* morning – as other travellers gathered around the jetty, a few pointing excitedly at the distant, thin, ornamental cityscape stitched across the horizon in which, somehow, three large white liners had got shipwrecked. It was ridiculous when you thought about it. Yes. *I was actually being paid to sit here waiting for a ferry to take me there. I was on my way to work*!

The surface of the lagoon was flashing with tongues of light and all kinds of boats and ships were hurrying back and forth in this busiest of waterways. I sat watching them most of the previous afternoon – a dredger, a Polish freighter, a police boat, an ocean-going crane, a pilot boat – all of them steaming past on their mysterious commercial errands and being watched both by me and the beady yellow eyes of a lone seagull sitting on top of a mooring pole sticking up out of the sea.

But the night was the best time to watch these ships as they came rearing up out of the darkness, silent and lit up like huge cathedrals of light, moving past with surprising speed and grace, given their size, before disappearing into a further darkness. Paul Theroux once wrote that he never heard a train without wanting to be on it and I've never seen a ship without wanting to be sitting on her aft deck. Whenever I saw a crew member standing in a vest and leaning on a ship's rail, I saw myself at a particularly lost and wild time in my life.

It came after I had left the sixth form in school and, in line with an early ambition to become a writer, I signed on with the merchant navy as an engineer steward on a Shaw Saville cargo boat sailing out of Liverpool and around Australia. I went around dressed in black, paperbacks stuffed in my pockets, not sure if I wanted to be Jack London, Henry Miller or Jean-Paul Sartre – or even a mixture of all three – but determined to write the great novel about something or other which would also, as a matter of course, upset the greatest number of people.

As a highly pretentious young intellectual I read voraciously, although my preferred meat and drink were the romantic revolutionary works of such as Jack Kerouac and all the beats, Henry Miller, Jack London, Lawrence Durrell, Ernest

Hemingway and Norman Mailer. I was, in a sense, a creation of all their wild romantic ideas and so it seemed just a normal career move for me to wander the world like London, educate myself in the ways of the docklands like Jean Genet, bed as many women as possible like Henry Miller and then write a string of novels which were also, with any luck, going to be totally disgusting.

But if that was a revolutionary career plan back in the 1950s, it is clearly quite normal now since the last paragraph might well be the intellectual template of almost any modern film-maker or playwright. They're all at it now. They are all in the persistent pursuit of the violent, the perverted, the melancholy and the cruel and I might well have stuck to the same path except for a truly pulverising few weeks in Malaya, where I was teaching with Voluntary Service Overseas after I graduated, and God broke through to me. He flung me against a wall, turned me inside out and told me he did not want me to carry on like that. Not only that, he also showed me clearly and unequivocally the havoc that artists like me were wreaking in his world. People like me had plunged his creation into an endless storm of black rain, he explained in an extremely vivid series of visions, and he would be extremely pleased if I stopped writing such things.

A lot of bridges have gone under the water since those stormy few weeks in Malaya and, for many years, particularly while I was working as a journalist in Fleet Street, I could only ever come to terms with that encounter with God by trying to pretend it had never happened. But whenever I see those big, deep-sea ships, such as those going into Venice harbour, I always think of those old wild, rebel dog days when I was setting out on my own literary career, first on that cargo boat and then a liner going around Africa, acting as you might expect a young Hemingway wannabe might act, often staggering home, bottle in hand, hoping, in the process, that some great book would somehow distil itself out of the gutter in which I so frequently found myself lying.

But then God made that devastating move on me in a conversion experience which began a more or less lifelong relationship with him. I gradually came to terms with what he seemed to be seeking from me, largely with the help of a few great men I met like the late Canon David Watson and Colonel Orde Dobbie. There were also friendships with Christian writers like Martin Wroe and Stewart Henderson and soon my life and relationship with God turned around completely.

Yet this relationship has never been easy or relaxed in the way that a lot of Christians seem to manage. There have been long periods when we haven't gone out together at all and I've pretty well fought God every inch of the way. And he's not been above a few odd counterpunches either.

It would all have been so much easier and more straightforward, I've often thought, if I'd ended up as an alcoholic writer, with a string of broken marriages behind me, writing pornography for lots of money in Hollywood. That's certainly the general direction in which I was heading as a merchant seaman until God invaded my life in Malaya.

I would have died of embarrassment in my days in the merchant navy had I been told I'd one day end up writing books about pilgrimages. *Pilgrimages*!

The water bus was crowded as we left Fusina and several small rainbows shimmered in our spray as it powered its way across the lagoon. A young Italian sitting in front of me offered me a cigarette and, almost without thinking about it, since I had certainly never done it before, I lifted the front of my T-shirt and showed the poor lad my operation scar. That's what you get when you smoke that, I indicated to him, pointing at his cigarettes and then at my red-raw pyjama case zipper. You are clearly mad, his face said, but he did put his cigarettes away again. I often wondered if that moment ever went on to have any impact on his dirty habit.

Everyone stood up excitedly as we drew up to the jetty which was almost directly opposite the porchway of a Basilica. I followed the others down a side street of old and wonky houses before we came down to another jetty where I caught a water bus up the Grand Canal. Loaded barges hurried this way and that across the marzipan-coloured water which lapped against the doorsteps of the baroque terraces. A huge water-borne jackhammer was pounding away at some pilings and the odd face looked down from the windows as we chugged along marvelling at the sheer improbability of it all. It was like travelling down a huge main road where all the traffic and asphalt had disappeared without trace under the sea. We might even have been journeying through a gigantic illusion with everything suspended on a big, miraculous cross-hatching of light and water. Occasionally there were sudden, enchanting views down watery side streets held together by nothing but the odd stone bridge.

We passed a few moving gondolas and a few more. The houses were clearly in an advanced geriatric condition – many had lost huge chunks of their plaster, others had walls bulging as if they were pregnant and the whole lot looked as if they were about to collapse, face first, straight into the drink at any moment. Also many of the stone columns looked as pock-marked as if they had recently been shelled. The bottoms of many of the doors had gone rotten too. You wouldn't have raised a £200 mortgage with the Abbey National on one of them.

The Rialto Bridge reared up high over us with many people on it, all gazing down in quiet amazement that the main road of any city in the world could be quite like this. The astonishing thing was that it was all even better than I had imagined and I got off the water bus at the Rialto with old received images booming around my brain along with the new. I saw that black coffin boat with the faces of Julie Christie and Donald Sutherland watching it moodily.

A man steering a speedboat with one hand while using the other to talk on a mobile zipped past adding to the suck and wash of the small waves on the doorsteps. MY SWEETHEART YOU ARE A MYSTERY SO I LIKE YOU, it said on the side of one of the water buses.

Venice has often been described as a place of barely suppressed carnality and I found myself thinking a lot about that sparkling Welsh writer Jan Morris with whom I had been corresponding recently. She thought that the city excited an emotion close to lust and I thought of Gustave von Aschenbach. What few lines have ever caught the bleak nature of a hopeless passion better than Thomas Mann's description of von Aschenbach following the Polish boy Tadzio in a gondola.

> Leaning back among soft, black cushions he swayed gently in the wake of the other black-snouted bark, to which the strength of his passion had chained him. Sometimes it passed from view and he was assailed by an anguish of unrest . . . the air was heavy and foul, the sun burnt down through the slate-coloured haze. Water slapped gurgling against wood and stone.

This was where Goethe first realized he had emerged from the darkness and grime of Northern Germany and finally got his first taste of the glorious light of the Italian Renaissance.

> As I glided over the lagoons in the brilliant sunshine and saw the gondoliers in their colourful costume, gracefully posed against the blue sky as they rowed with easy strokes across the light-green surface of the water, I felt I was looking at the latest and best painting of the Venetian school.

Ernest Hemingway, Henry James and Somerset Maugham have also stood on this spot on the Rialto, although I suppose Venice will always belong to Lord Byron who raised hell here for a while with his flock of mistresses, carousing until dawn with Shelley and the pair of them swimming the length of the canal at midnight. Byron especially liked the way dusty shadows patched the Rialto at night. Shakespeare's Shylock also had his shop on this bridge, although I'd better not make too much of that after my ravings in Verona.

The city wasn't even particularly smelly or dirty, as I had often been warned – the odd, drainy whiff for sure but the breezes bouncing in off the sea ensured a certain freshness almost everywhere you wandered. You could even see a few feet down into the marzipan water and, all around one huge vegetable boat, I spotted hundreds of small fish feeding. I also found lichen on a few tombstones, a sign of little pollution if ever there was one.

The sheer volume of traffic on the canal was another surprise: mostly loaded barges reminding you that this was not just a tourist city with literary ghosts but a working, living city. People were sitting on the stone steps of the Rialto with their feet cooling in the water. Gondoliers importuned for business, offering 'special prices'. There was an old Welsh story I've always liked about the meeting of a town council and a discussion about what to do with a new lake. Why not put some gondolas on it, one councillor suggested. A good idea, said another, but how many? Well, why don't we start with a pair, piped up another, and we'll see how well they breed.

Most of the shops around the Rialto were selling elaborate face masks which all, well, smiled at you with big, hooked noses and eyeless eyes. Tourists were milling everywhere – hundreds, if not thousands, of them crowding the small alleyways where they could buy from vivid piles of sun-drenched fruit, pick from slippery piles of fish, prawns and squid or try a slice of coconut kept wet and cold in a small water fountain. There were also old prints of maps of the city and T-shirts with Botticelli cherubs or midnight views of the city. WE SEND ALL OVER THE WORLD.

I bought a lovely leather-bound notebook with handmade paper. It cost me Regent Street, Oxford Street and all my hotels but I was well pleased with it and sat on a ledge for a while just smoothing it with my palms. It was only later I saw the real defect in it which was that I couldn't imagine any of my thoughts ever being sufficiently Aristotelian to deface its lovely pages with. I would reserve it only for brilliant aphorisms, I thought, which is why it remains as empty as when I first bought it.

Many of the tourists weren't their country's best exports: mostly rich Americans, I judged, with vastly overweight women who smoked before and after every course in the restaurants and the men whose vain toupees were being gradually and visibly separated from their foreheads by the *sweat* on their foreheads. Aschenbach again – aka Dirk Bogarde – the black dye from his hair running down over his furrowed features as they disinfected the squares with the onset of a smallpox epidemic. There were also some beautifully coiffed, young European girls hand in hand with elderly men with bellies like Alpine landslips. Moving through all this was an English nerd wearing a Manchester United team strip. You could always pick out the locals too, usually quietly but immaculately dressed, their body language stiff with a pained forbearance that they had to put up with all this rabble if only because they paid the bills.

Yet the city remained so marvellous in her promise, so fresh in her sea breezes and so magical in her spirit, that she seemed to float on some mysterious hammock of water and light, all these crowds, with their multi-tongued babble, did not intrude. Venice transcended them all.

The back alleys were the best: shadowy places, full of marzipan water lapping on crumbling brick, where little children chased the pigeons around the small squares and artists stood on even smaller bridges trying to capture the moment in poses which presumably served them well when they were trying to chat up impressionable young girls. Everywhere you looked – and from almost every angle – there was an Impressionist masterpiece hanging right there in the air.

You would, however, need a lot more than Park Lane or Oxford Circus to catch a ride in one of those gondolas and I spent an enjoyable ten minutes leaning on a parapet of a bridge and watching at least seven of them who all seemed to have gone and got themselves stuck in a gondola jam with a lot of unseemly cussing going on, some shouting accusations about how the other would never make a decent gondolier as long as he had a nose on his face. The row just got worse – as did the jam – and I did feel a little sympathy for the couples just sitting there who had forked out something like £100 for a magical moment of love in a Venetian gondola and there they were stuck in the middle of a noisy eisteddfod of oars and cusses.

The city also had a dazzling collection of churches which I walked around like a faithful and dutiful pilgrim doing his Stations of the Cross. Not that I tried to swallow them whole or buy fat guide books to swot up on the Byzantine fiddles or Corinthian conceits. I just wandered inside them and tried to absorb their personalities, feel a little of their old poetry or the warmth of a living faith. There was one Basilica which had been inspired by a dream of doves and flowers; another had a whole forest of statues and yet another contained the tombs of the old Doges. You never really knew what you were going to stumble across next as you left the sunny hurly burly of the street and entered these caverns of medieval shadows, usually lit only by glimmering banks of smoking candles or whatever sunshine managed to wheedle its way down through the stained glass.

In retrospect it was all a bit like wandering through a strange, dark dream in which a candle occasionally illuminated an ancient sarcophagus or an impossibly ornate altar or even a Titian or Tintoretto. You could almost say that there was the very throb of God in all those old, crumbling churches: a serene, mature God, no longer given to tantrums and immensely satisfied with the generations of artistry which had been put in to his continuing glory. Immerse yourself in it all and you know it just can't all have been for nothing.

God always needs to look at great art, you feel, just as he always needs to listen to believing prayer. They are his staple diets and, without them, he can become angry and even dangerous.

But perhaps there is always a dark side to even the most beautiful face as I found out that night back in Fusina when the massed ranks of mosquitoes, midges and moths, not forgetting a horrible little green thing the shape of a Stealth Bomber, came bundling through my camper door as soon as darkness fell. I had left the door open and fallen asleep over my notebook.

They must have been breeding in the sea and can't have had a square meal for weeks since they all duly began setting about me, if not exactly with knife and fork then certainly with great relish. I jumped up and told them straight I didn't want their types in here and duly began setting about them with an excellent, noxious spray, which I always keep at the ready to greet such unwanted guests. When I had finished them all off they were lying around on their backs mostly next to my stove with their little legs poking up stiffly into the air. Lovely.

I have no sentiment about such things. Many drugs tests have never found a trace of Buddhism in my spiritual blood.

Once they get into my camper they'll hide away for hours or even weeks before getting you, usually in the middle of the night when you're fast asleep. I picked up one mosquito on a pilgrimage to Santiago de Compostela and, despite all my best efforts, he woke up every few days and bit me all the way there and all the way back again. But now I've got sprays. Lots and lots of noxious sprays.

An old friend returned to me in a series of lively dreams that night: the coelacanth. But he wasn't standing on his head in the sea outside his cave this time and had brought along two of his mates. The three of them were the right side up and dancing back and forth together, all of them, bizarrely, even by the bizarre standards of my bizarre dreams, wearing coloured Hawaiian grass skirts.

I returned to Venice the next day on the same water bus to visit the main focus of my pilgrimage here – the great Basilica of San Marco which contains the body of St Mark. This morning I went in the other direction down the Grand Canal and, even given what I had already seen in this miraculous city, I was still unprepared for what I saw next. We came out into a huge lagoon surrounded distantly by temples and basilicas which again all seemed to have been erected on the improbable foundations of light and water. The buildings were also wreathed in creamy wisps of mist and I don't suppose I have ever seen a sight which was so real and unreal at the same time. In fact I'm still not quite sure I've actually seen it. Even as I try and picture this lagoon it still seems a strange and misty dream.

The crowds were already up and about, doing what crowds do, and I passed a line of hawkers before coming out onto St Mark's Square, a huge piazza bordered on three sides by arcades and which Napoleon once called the finest drawing room in Europe. Pigeons and tourists vied for food and fun in front of the shops with jewels in their windows which twinkled with ferocious expense. A full orchestra was playing in front of one of the restaurants – a rousing theme which explored something along the lines of enjoy yourself now because you are going to die of shock when you learn what we are going to charge you for a cup of coffee before you leave.

And there it was on my right, the actual church which I had read so much about – the mighty Basilica of San Marco – not really terribly mighty now I had come face to face with her, more an exquisitely pretty collection of Russian Orthodox domes, lonely statues and minarets, all forming a tricky Byzantine poem which was so small and highly wrought you wanted to pick it all up, put it in your pocket and take it home. The more you gazed at the façade the more intricate it became with delicate frescoes under many of the arches and four life-size bronze horses directly above the main door. But even the main door, when you came to take a closer look, wasn't so much one door as a dozen of them all mashed up together. Those architects would never use one door when a dozen would do.

My first reaction to it was amusement which soon turned to a slight bewilderment. John Ruskin thought that it was not only 'a symbol of the redeemed church of God' but also 'a book of prayer, a miniature parchment on which the Divine Word is written'. Indeed, no city had ever had 'a more glorious Bible'. But I wasn't with him on that one. The Basilica of San Marco was too theatrical to be a proper church. Everything was just too fussy, too overworked and even Disneyesque. You couldn't really worship inside somewhere like that: all you'd want to do inside somewhere like that is eat popcorn or burst out laughing. Give me an old Welsh chapel on a bare, sheep-littered hill any day of the week.

My growing feelings of antagonism towards the place were then considerably thickened by the haphazard and confusing queues spilling out of various doors. Not that I am opposed to queues as such: just that I noticed the group tours were being moved straight in through one door while we plebs were barely moving through another.

But then my morning brightened considerably when I began chatting with a forty-something doctor from Sydney, Mary Webber, over here with a friend and 'doing Europe'. The trouble was her friend didn't like doing any of the 'arty' stuff and had gone off to look at the Venice Film Festival, which was on at the time, leaving Mary to do the pictures and churches.

Mary spoke fast and loud in the usual harshly strangulated vowels of her race and never minced her words. She also clearly loved any form of art and, when I confessed to not knowing a lot about Caravaggio, she practically frogmarched me into a bookshop, picked up a book on the man, which she had no intention of buying, and took me through her favourite paintings page by page while also explaining what was so special about Caravaggio's work – the development of personality, the telling psychological penetration, the novel use of light and perspective.

She was also rather beefy and looked as though she might pack a good punch so I tucked in right behind her as she waded through the crowds in the Basilica of San Marco rather like Moses parting the Dead Sea. Not that we got too far since there was a turnstile on the main aisle, where we had to pay up another wedge of lira and, almost immediately, another cash desk where we had to fork out yet another to get into the Treasury. We paid up like good tourists but Mary was already getting narked. 'It's worse than American motorways where they nickle and dime you all the time.'

The contents of the Treasury were a moderately interesting collection of works in silver, gold and crystal – together with the usual collection of 'bones' – although the guide on our tape machines explained that most of the precious stones and pearls had been sold off to pay for the church restoration in the last century, which is not what you want to hear *after* you've paid to get in there. We were also most amused to learn that most of the exhibits had been 'stolen' from the Turks in Constantinople even if the word used was always 'recovered'.

'Ah, those poor old Turks,' Mary sighed. 'It's no wonder they've got nothing today when everything's been nicked off them.'

Whereas the governments of today are often moved to war over oil or an oppressive dictator, they would often have a good war in medieval times over a saint's body. Venice, once the financial capital of Europe, with the best navy in the world, plundered all kinds of bodies and holy relics from all over. Apart from Mark they also got the hand of John the Baptist and the body of his father Zacharia; they also pinched Stephen from Constantinople and managed to make off with the bodies of San Isidoro and San Donato.

Mark's body was actually stolen from Alexandria and secreted inside a large basket of herbs and pork. The carriers were told to keep shouting 'Pork!' in case any Muslims might be inclined to want to ask questions or search the basket. When they got to the port the body was hidden in the sails and hung off the mast to avoid any further searches. A fierce storm broke out after the ship sailed, whereupon Mark appeared before the captain and advised him to strike the sails or they would hit a hidden bank. The captain took this advice and his ship was duly saved. Or so the story goes.

One definite hazard of being in Mary Webber's company, I soon discovered, was her burning need to touch everything. She was forever looking around furtively to see if a peaked cap was about before reaching out to touch this or smooth that. 'It's just an Australia thing,' she explained. 'We like to be rebellious. We like to rub up officialdom.'

The basilica's interior was quite extraordinary with almost every wall and roof covered in a gold mosaic and various coloured tableaux. Marble pillars supported a series of arches, all glittering in a dull Ali Baba way although, as we were up in the gallery studying them, it was Mary who pointed out that all of them were out of true. And they were. Maybe this Basilica was sinking into the sea faster than anyone has yet thought but not one of those golden arches was in line with one another. Every building line was out of whack.

Indeed, the irregular oddity of the place stayed in my mind for a long time and I never really came to terms with it; never quite understood what this glittering golden palace was all about. Théophile Gautier thought it belonged to a pre-Christian Christianity, to a church founded before religion existed.

The view from the balcony outside was marvellous, full of shimmering light, ships moving across the lagoon and wheeling pigeons, one of which got me right on my bald patch. 'It'll bring you luck,' a black American laughed as he handed me a Kleenex.

I lost Mary for a while only to find her again cuddling one of the bronze horses. 'You're going to get your hands chopped off one day,' I warned her.

'I just can't help it. I see these things and have to hold them. When I hold them they become a part of me forever.'

Once back inside we attached ourselves to another queue waiting to go up to the altar and have a close look at the famous huge, golden altarpiece which can be turned around for a service. 'Oh, look it's bringing out my nascent Catholicism,' Mary said only to change tack immediately and start wondering how difficult it might be to steal it because it must have been worth millions. We put some more money into a wall guide to get the full picture on the altarpiece and were again amused to learn that they had also stolen this treasure from the Turks.

And there he was at last, resting inside a golden casket directly in front of us on the High Altar. St Mark. The casket wasn't sectioned off by ropes or anything and Mary took a quick look around before bounding up there. For one horrifying moment I thought she was going to try and open the casket to give Mark a quick cuddle but all she did was lay her hands on it.

Then, even after all my snooty warnings, I was right up after her by her side and there we were – the Aussie quack and the Welsh hack – both of us smiling at one another as our hands rested on the coffin of St Mark.

I had been doing well for saints lately – what with Luke and a possible Matthew in Padua but Mark means more to me than almost all of them. The Pope hasn't heard about this but, for me, Mark has always been the patron saint of journalists. He was – no argument about it – the best reporter of them all.

A friend and companion of Peter and Paul, as well as one of the disciples, Mark wrote his Gospel at a time when all the eyewitnesses to the life of Christ were being killed or were dying. His account was the first to be published and formed the basis of the Gospels of Matthew and Luke. In essence, his witness was direct and simple reportage, written with narrative pace, dramatic detail and a bare economy of style. The stories gradually present a clear account of the public life of Jesus leading steadily to the climax of the Crucifixion.

The personality of Jesus rings out through the story as clear and clean as steel, and the last three chapters tell how Jesus was arrested, tried and killed in one continuous narrative. We see, in Mark's account, the story of a man who, in the words of Albert Schweitzer, 'bent history to his purpose, flung himself upon the wheel of the world. It crushed him but he hangs there still. That is his victory.'

The striking stylistic feature of his narrative is that the identity of Jesus as Messiah is kept secret right to the end. We are only given the facts, from which we may draw our own conclusions. Jesus reveals himself in what he says and does. We are also spared the views and personality of the author.

Mark left himself out of the story completely although he *may* have referred to himself once as 'the young man who fled naked from the Garden of Gethsemane at the time of Jesus' arrest'.

The Gospel is the work of a great reporter and a master of good writing who was lucky enough to get turned loose on the biggest assignment in history. And there I was, that autumnal day in 1999, in Venice, in the Basilica of San Marco, with an Aussie doctor, both of us smiling at one another as our hands *rested on his coffin*, making St Mark a part of us forever.

There was a moment later that day when the character of this basilica'd city seemed to change within the chrysalis of a light yellow sunset. Whole streets seemed to empty of the milling throngs, as if the last tourist had left on the last bus. You could stand on the stone bridges and actually hear the water lapping in the darkness. Lovers slipped past, hand in hand, through the tangled shadows and, down on the waterfront, the warm night air filled with the odd throaty song of a gondolier.

The gondolas crossed and re-crossed the lagoon with their lamps dangling in the darkness like giant glow-worms. Orange and white light settled on the water in streaks and patches. Accordion music hung in the lamplight of one corner and I sat on a wooden box watching the domes and spires of the basilicas taking up ancient postures against a sky which had gone from yellow to light blue and was now deepening into a dark purple. Odd lights came on in odd living rooms with dark silhouettes of people coming out onto the balconies of their *palazzos*, standing in their own light and taking in a little air before withdrawing again like night spiders.

It had been a long day and I was tired now, after tasting so many of the city's endless delights, and I finally left my wooden box to find my way back to the Fusina ferry. Yet the city grid never seemed to make any sense as I took wrong turnings down darkened alleyways, often ending up on the same bridges I had just left or coming out against the dead ends of old walls with gargoyled fountains.

But tired as I was, I felt no anxiety in all this strange, ruined darkness, just a continuing wonder really, stopping to touch an old door knocker or run my fingertips along a wall, asking myself if Marco Polo might have walked down this very alleyway, smoothed this very door or even drunk out of that very fountain. I might even have found some dark corner and settled down to sleep right there. It was warm enough but the occasional nip told of insects abroad – which might also account for the emptiness of the streets – and I hadn't brought my arsenal of noxious sprays. There were certainly enough moths fluttering in the light of the street lamps.

The insides of many of the restaurants were full of people and laughter as the waiters glided from table to table. A cat wandered through the table legs of one, looking and sniffing around for any juicy droppings, and a table of diners roared in appreciation as a waiter brought something on a tray which resembled a dozen sparklers on bonfire night. Their joy made me feel lonely and wanting to go home.

Only a few gondolas were still out on the water when the ferry chugged back to Fusina and the huge hoot of a ship's horn blared fatly into the night. I was so tired by now I could have slept on a washing line. I could barely speak let alone inspect the extremely lengthy line of the day's Venetian corpses. I only hoped that after this long, strange day, with the spirit of St Mark curled up and asleep on my lap, I could have a decent night's sleep myself, untroubled by mad dreams of dancing coelacanths or loud bangs on my camper in the middle of the night.

CHAPTER 8

A Florentine Sunday

The city of Florence lies scattered over a wide flat plain with spires, bell towers and basilica domes rising up over her plum-red roofs and dull cream walls. Mountains lined with parasols of pines come trooping down to her outskirts and, way beyond the immediate mountains, are yet more mountains. They were blue and dark were these mountains, slipping around one another like the big backs of hunting whales in the Atlantic. It really was a vista of ancient grandeur with angels wandering over the mountains and making their ways over the flat plains to spend a day in a city held together by a pristine passion, all sitting there waiting for a new Leonardo to come and set up his easel.

The sun was rising through a bank of autumnal mist behind me, darkening the plum rooftops while also giving those cream walls a pattern of luminescent and hopeful gold. Deep within all the buildings you could pick out the formal shapes of gardens and even the tower which once housed Galileo's telescope. But then, if you peered even closer, you could make out hidden gardens of geraniums and vines in the roofs. He would be a blessed person indeed who could wake up every morning and sit high on his own geranium terrace watching the sun rise up over his own home in Florence.

The River Arno curved around the side of the city, moving slowly under three or four medieval stone bridges. The brown water seemed to keep attracting and holding the morning light to it although, occasionally, you spotted a long, silver flash which might be fish feeding and turning over their silver bellies in the weeds. The domes of the basilicas hovered above the houses like Stone Age flying saucers waiting for permission to land. Some of the domes were a tawny brown although one was green.

It was only as I stood standing here gazing down at the opulent and sunny gorgeousness of this, the City of Flowers, that I realized that *all* the high buildings were ecclesiastical. These people have actually built their homes beneath their churches and not the other way around. A beautiful old church dominates almost every view in this part of the world and you can often feel the very air around them trembling with believing prayer.

I passed Bologna the other day and the huge Basilica there was practically a mountain itself, perched high on top of another mountain. It just sat there telling everyone who cared to look, with raw passion and silhouetted eloquence, how these people have always lived in the fear of God. Let no dog bark when I speak my name, that basilica in Bologna said. Shade your eyes. Watch your step or you'll have the Pope on your tail.

This glorious autumn, on the very eve of a new millennium, seemed to be getting brighter and warmer with every new dawn. There was still no sign of it breaking down into a cold winter and, camped high on the hillside overlooking Florence, just next to the Piazzale Michelangelo, I was again feasting on pilgrim delights and feeling that God was laying out each of my mornings as an invitation to a wonderful feast. Each successive day was ringing in my mind like a perfectly ascending series of musical notes all played out on an endless platform of autumnal sunshine. On the pilgrim road to Compostela two years earlier I was always being savaged by hungry insects or ending up in concealed ditches. And it had rained pretty much every day too – unlike the high, breaking wave of this wonderful autumn without end.

If you want to get the real feel of a city go alone and very early, I have always thought. Go with respect in your heart, cap in hand and with your hair combed properly long before anyone else has got up. Knock on her door while everyone is still in dreamland and slip into her boudoir without making any noise so that you can gaze on her face without the concealing benefits of lots of make-up. See her in her pyjamas with her eyes thick with sleep and her hair all over the place. And only *then* will you get the real feel of a city.

And so it was that, early that Sunday morning, I found myself being followed only by my own lonely footfalls as I made my way along the tall, dark canyons of those thin Florentine streets. It was too early even for the bells, and the iron manhole covers declared that they were the property of the Commune di Firenze, Fognatoro. A few drifts of litter here and there but not much. Most of the cobbled streets had evidently been hosed down overnight.

I walked along the Via Dei Bentaccordi and, with the low-lying sun still yet to penetrate the street's darkness, was enjoying the silence when I came across an old man, shoulder leaning against a wall and coughing his heart up. It was a pitiful sight as, with each long, rackety cough, his spitting tongue flickered out like an adder's. Perhaps predictably, he was also holding a cigarette in one hand and waiting to stop coughing before taking another drag.

A few of those cursed mopeds were also up and about with their high-pitched whines and exhausts letting out blue puffs of smoke. A burst of bells rang out. The peal was short when another came from another part of the city, duelling for only a minute or so before they both stopped. The front doors were old and crumbling with as many different door knobs as there are weeds in a field. A snatch of violin music came and went.

A lone dog was out sniffing corners and taking his morning walk when, down on the next corner, I came across an empty wine bottle in a basket hanging on the end of a long piece of rope. The other end of the rope disappeared over a window sill about three storeys up.

We normal people usually have milk or bread delivered first thing in the morning and I smiled at the thought of someone lying in bed up there, unable to sleep and waiting with some impatience for the delivery of a fresh bottle of wine so that he might get back to sleep again. He would be a failed poet, I fancied, down on his luck and flush out of doggerel, with barely the energy or will to get out of bed any longer and just waiting to die in the ever-deepening puddle of his own alcoholic self-pity.

The huge, colourless square in front of Santa Croce Church was deserted except for a man walking his dog and quite a few maurauding pigeons. The church doors were open and, inside, I found a sprinkling of old women with their handbags down on their knees in one of the chapels for the first service of the morning. Where would any of our churches be without old women and their handbags?

The nave was a bit of a mess with scaffolding and sheets of polythene draped over most everything, but a quiet wander around the many tombstones, chapels and memorials was a little like a quiet wander through some of the brighter moments of Italian history. Here was a memorial to Marconi and over there was Dante, no longer making a minute examination of the topography of hell. Machiavelli was no longer essaying visions of political savagery either because he was inside that sarcophagus there and even the great Michelangelo was no longer dazzling everyone with his art since he was lying in that tomb, brought to Florence after one of the greatest and most elaborate funerals of the Renaissance.

Just here at the entrance was a bust of Galileo, flanked by the Muses of Astronomy and Geometry, holding a telescope with one hand as the other rested on a globe of the world. It is a clever tableau representing the great range of this man's life – stargazer, moon-watcher, lens grinder, mathematician and troublemaker *extraordinaire*.

He had so vexed the Pope with his interpretation of the movements of the universe that his body was originally brought here to Santa Croce and put away in a discreet side chapel. But as it gradually dawned on a stupid world that, not for the first time, they had denounced a man for being right all along, he was soon brought out of the chapel and put in this rather more public place albeit without one of his vertebrae, three fingers from his right hand and one of his teeth. They might have been earmarked as future 'pigges' bones' but what actually did happen to them I never did find out.

As a brilliant collection of corpses they simply didn't come any more brilliant than those assembled at Santa Croce and I saw then how a great church can become a remembrancer of her people; how the church can gather together all that is fine in national life and then continually mediate all this illustrious achievement to her flock. You too can rise above the ordinary and be someone, all those corpses were telling us still. You too can make a mark.

In another chapel I watched the sunlight falling directly on the altar as a priest prayed alone. His prayer was clearly as fervent as believing prayer gets and I could almost see his words riding up that staircase of sunlight on the altar and then travelling directly into the ears of God. If God has a telephone, the actual lines can only be made of sunlight. But most of what he hears must give him earache when, more often than not, he is prone to bang down the receiver. God is no good at pretending to listen to what he doesn't want to hear. Tetchy. Irascible. That's often him. The grandfather you never quite understand and even fear even if you do always implicitly accept the basic goodness of his heart.

I also lingered for a while over the Giotto frescoes which first told the people about the life of St Francis. Those didactic images were the very first teachers of the Florentine poor. Even those who couldn't read could understand them.

Outside in the square a few more people were moving about and a trader with a long pigtail was setting up his souvenir stall. A shop called The Gold Corner was well and truly shuttered, as you might expect a gold corner to be, and more bells rang out briefly only to fall silent again. The Pope's men used to burn books and heretics out in this square during the Inquisition which must have livened it up no end because, you would have to say, this might be one of the dullest squares anywhere. Even the old Communist squares in the old German Democratic Republic were far more interesting than this one. At least the Communists like to put nice, big fountains in their squares and all this one had was a few tatty souvenir stalls.

The sun had cranked herself up a good few more feet as I crossed the square and followed a few more high, dark alleyways before coming out into the gathering brightness of the Piazza della Signoria. This square is said to represent both the heart of Florence and the light of the Renaissance and more than a few writers have gone on about the symbolic nature of the walk when you follow the darkness of the alleys before coming out into the light of this famous square.

Many of the greatest painters, mathematicians, astronomers and philosophers in the history of the world have walked across this square but again squares don't come much more boring than this square, a most bland square of buildings with tall, square faces and yet more pigeons pecking around the tyres of a line of police cars parked next to the Palazzo Vecchio.

It did, however, have a wonderfully baroque statue of Neptune with water falling all around him, picking up the sunlight everywhere and making it dance. And just over the way was a copy of the tall, white statue of Michelangelo's David, all Weetabix muscles and testosterone calves and so flagrantly and defiantly masculine he has become something of a gay icon. The Grand Duke of Cosimo was also here, astride a horse with both his front hooves raised off the plinth which, I think, recalling the answer in some distant quiz show, means that he died in battle. Or maybe it was in bed.

Directly in front of Neptune was a huge, brick building, The Generali, now completely costumed in sunlight. Many of the high, surrounding verandahs had vines growing on them and most stone ledges had a pigeon or three watching the morning unfold beneath them. A small woman was pushing a huge pile of luggage on wheels. 'There are no buses,' she said in English in reply to my curious stare.

I walked across the square and went down another deserted alleyway, the Via Dello Studio, when the side of a huge dome reared up over me like an artificial eyebrow. Not any old dome either but The Dome – Duomo – the largest and highest cupola of its day, floating in the Florentine sky with effortless majesty.

When the architect, Filippo Brunelleschi, announced he was going to build such a huge dome, without any scaffolding, no one believed it could be done and their scepticism increased when he refused to say how he was going to do it. Yet, after work lasting 14 years, he did do it and still no one quite understands how it stays up there.

They say that the whole cathedral cost eighteen million gold florins and took 175 years to build and you have to believe them. But when I stood there looking up at this wonderfully dotty exterior, full of white, green and red marble panels, all I could do was think of E. M. Forster's line when he said: 'There is something majestic about the bad taste of Italy.'

Inside the faithful had already finished the first service of the morning and candles were still burning on one of the chapel altars. By now the sun had also set one of the stained glass windows ablaze with light and, in it, you could see the shadows of pigeons messing about outside. In the aisle a priest was counselling a young woman who was wringing her hands wretchedly. Even in her distress she had a lively beauty about her with long, curly hair, light, brown skin and blackberry eyes. What trouble, you wondered, had she gone and got herself into? The same trouble that usually befalls beautiful young women everywhere, you guess, and almost certainly something to do with a beautiful young man.

And again inside this church we find testimony to all the richness and plenitude of life on earth in the faded frescoes and suffering Madonnas; in the geometric and zodiacal motifs, the squadrons of stone angels and in the blood-curdling visions of hell in some of the frescoes. There were posturing statues, yet more tombs and a crypt which smelled of mildew and damp. You could spend your whole life studying every corner of this place and then only get half of it. They have even, they say, got the jaw of Jerome and the index finger of John the Baptist in the museum.

The seriously strange Savonarola once ruled the pulpit in here in Duomo, fiercely denouncing the growing doctrine of humanism and warning everyone of the terrible punishment that awaited them if they turned their backs on God. He even savaged Botticelli for painting nudes so fiercely the old master agreed to change his ways, although the particular speciality of this Ayatollah of ice and fire was attacking finery, greed and gambling, calling for a return to a puritan simplicity. To this end he arranged a bonfire each year on the Piazza della Signoria on which everyone was invited to fling their playing cards, wigs, scents, make-up, fine dresses – the Bonfire of the Vanities.

Unfortunately the fickle Florentines turned on him in the

end and flung him on a real bonfire, first stringing him up in the same Piazza, burning his corpse then throwing the ashes on the river on which they then exploded some gunpowder just to make sure. You can find an extremely small memorial plaque to him in the Piazza if you look carefully enough.

Back outside I was gazing into the dancing heart of yet another fountain when there was movement inside it; something odd in the whirling light with the figure of a man turning slowly and fixing me with a forensic look. His beard was grey and forehead high with a sparkly intelligence. He wore a simple brown gown with a plain white collar to disguise the complex patterns of his mind. I almost stood to attention as he kept looking at me – Florence's most famous son, a man with the brain the size of a garage which kept vibrating with so many insights and ideas he became the leading figure of the Italian Renaissance and the Father of the Age of Reason.

He was actually born in Pisa but grew up here in Florence, soon announcing himself as different from the rest in his obsessions with such as pendulums and falling bodies; compasses and water clocks. He also studied tides, river flows, the diffusion of light and the acceleration of matter. He watched comets with his telescope and was the first to find sunspots, which he likened to the dark tears in the heart of God. But he enjoyed and celebrated human things too – the love of his eldest daughter, fixing broken clocks and growing oranges from seed in terracotta pots.

His was a tough, harsh world though, full of Inquisition spies and plague germs to the extent that Florentines would often carry a wooden Madonna through these very streets in an effort to ward off the plague which was wiping out household after household.

But whereas most people worried where the plague would strike next, Galileo mostly worried about how the heavens actually went around. By 1597 he had decided that the system of Copernicus was true and that of Ptolemy was false. We were not, in fact, the centre of the universe. We revolved within a revolving planetary system. We were always on the move. We were all of us clinging – just – to a rogue star. He wrote:

> The moons revolving around Jupiter, the mountains and craters of the moon, the waxing and waning of Venus, the strange appearance of Saturn, the passage of comets, the appearance and disappearance of stars and the movements of sunspots. All these make the Copernican system so much more likely than the Ptolemaic system.

Yet, as Luther had already discovered to his painful cost, these were hard times for freethinkers, particularly when such thoughts were bounced up against the high, hard wall of the Vatican. The Pope believed Copernicus contradicted key passages in the Bible and one Bishop called for Copernicus to be imprisoned, clearly unaware he had already been dead for all of 70 years.

Rogue philosophers were still liable to be clapped in irons, extensively tortured, stoned to death in public, burned at the stake or even broken on a wheel. You thought what the Pope wanted you to think or it was the big chop. But Galileo insisted on following the dictates of his own reason and research. Good philosophers fly alone like the eagle, he wrote. Not in flocks like starlings who fill the skies with shrieks and cries.

So he pressed ahead composing a long letter on the relation of astronomy to Scripture in which he argued the liberal use of the principle of accommodation in interpreting biblical passages apparently inconsistent with the motion of the earth. Then real trouble started brewing in 1616 when theologians in the Holy Office asserted that to maintain the immobility of the earth was heretical and Copernicus was placed on the index of banned books pending correction.

Galileo was told of this but he nevertheless pressed ahead and wrote his famous *Dialogues*, his examination of the movements of the heavens, here in Florence. He was under the impression he was able to discuss the new system provided it was offered merely as a hypothesis and he did not introduce any biblical arguments. The book involved him in a momentous struggle: getting permission from the Pope to start it, actually penning it and then obtaining a licence to print it. But he always thought he was safe enough. There was nothing anti-religious in it, he said. 'The Bible shows the way to go to heaven, not the way the heavens go.'

Unfortunately for Galileo the Jesuits hated the book and the Pope went ballistic too. This fool from Florence had meddled where he had been told not to meddle. He had thought for himself, damn his brain. Divine power can never be limited by the narrow compass of human understanding. Who did he think he was?

Galileo was duly summoned to explain himself before the Inquisition in Rome before the end of October. Full of arthritis, sciatica and several other ailments, he claimed he was in a 'pitiable state of bodily indisposition' and couldn't go. But they weren't having it. Either you come or you'll be clapped in irons and dragged here – *and at your own expense.*

And so it was that the stage was set for the trial of the heretic Galileo in Rome; a trial which came to represent a clash between the individual and authority; the fight between modern radicalism and ancient beliefs; the struggle between science and religion which, 500 years later, shows no sign of abating.

I stayed in Florence for three days, deciding to get up extremely early again the next morning so that I could beard the Uffizi Art Gallery alone. I would buy a few croissants for breakfast and share them with the pigeons on the steps of the Uffizi, I thought as I strolled through another golden dawn on the banks of the Arno. I might even splash out on a cappuccino and just sit there watching the morning come together.

But I couldn't have misjudged the situation more completely – even two hours before opening there was already a queue a mile long, stretching out of the courtyard and down along the river. Had I got there an hour later I would have ended up somewhere back in France. Most of the others in the queue were Japanese, I noted: a race who don't seem to need any sleep unless they all go to bed at eight o'clock the night before.

And with the tourists came the usual camp followers: the postcard sellers and the beggars with their hands held out, the female sellers of icons and rosaries, the pickpockets and the street photographers, the caricaturists and the silhouettists and the African sellers of prints of the old masters who, you guessed, probably made more in a week than the old masters made in a lifetime. Occasionally the police appeared and a lot of the hawkers disappeared but mostly they continued circling you like cinematic Red Indians looking for weaknesses in the defences of your circled wagons before making their attack.

The queue wasn't moving at all and I began chatting with the man next to me only to discover that we had last seen one another 40 years ago when we had been in the same class in a grammar school in Cardiff. He was David Bravery, now a London engineer, and it was a lovely half an hour, with his Austrian wife looking on bemusedly, as we reminisced on those teachers we loved and those we hated – Ernie Brookes who could hit you with a lump of chalk from any distance, Capo Thomas who put you in detention for breathing and Smudge, the gym master, who would either fell you with one mighty blow or grab you and give you a big kiss. Oh yes, and what happened to . . . ?

The Uffizi paintings were as inspiring as you might hope with an art gallery which is billed as one of the greatest in the world – many of them visions of beauty painted in the pure, clean light of the Renaissance. It is impossible on such visits to take in much but I lingered over Giotto's Madonna, Fra Angelico's Coronation of the Virgin, da Vinci's Adoration of the Magi, Michelangelo's Holy Family, Titian's Flora and just about everything by Botticelli whose female sitters, particularly in The Birth of Venus, seem more ravishingly and mysteriously beautiful than any women I have seen anywhere.

Those paintings floated through my mind like leaves before an uncertain wind for days and even weeks. Most all of them had a religious connection and what did occur as I stood in front of them was how the artists of old must have held society together with the centrality and certainty of their religious visions. They also fashioned the key features and ideas of what was to become the Renaissance, a time when man stepped out of the shadow of received dogma and found his own human face and form. Heaven and earth are made for man but man is made for himself, said Latini. God in Christ is accessible and is one of us on earth, said St Francis. Real life can be created from dead matter. These are all Renaissance ideas.

And yet, following on all this, I couldn't also but help think of that sad exhibition in the Royal Academy in London the previous year, *Sensations*, when we were presented with a head moulded from the artist's own blood, a portrait of a bullet hole, mutilated children engaged in perverted sex, cut-up animals, quartered sharks and a portrait of the Moors murderer Myra Hindley made from the handprints of small children.

Such art tells us much about the cancerous visions of the modern artist; of how he has completely lost his way and, unable to resonate with the real world, is now peddling his sick and squalid nightmares. And in the context of the work in the Uffizi, that exhibition tells us much about our modern darkness too; of how, where we were once presented with beauty and faith, we are now routinely presented with violence, cruelty and perversion. Where artists once brought the liberating light of the Renaissance they now offer the imprisoning darkness of their own sickness. We are valueless, alone and cast out. Or, as Beckett had it, he doesn't exist, the bastard.

The reactions of visitors to Florence have been many and varied. Robert Browning hymned the city's continual delight and charm while Laurie Lee spoke of 'carved palaces which quivered like radiators in the sun' and 'brick-faced tourists sweating and counting their crumpled money'. Dylan Thomas didn't like it at all, describing it as a 'gruelling museum'. He was, he said, 'sick of drinking chianti in a marble shanty, sick of vini and contadini and bambini'.

For myself I warmed to the art and churches but was happy to make my final escape since, unlike Venice, you never seemed to be able to avoid the traffic or the tourists. The nights were the worst, when the narrow, medieval streets throbbed with a warmed-up soup of diesel exhaust and body odour. They were not the usual traffic jams which moved every half an hour but traffic jams which seemed to move not at all, with men even tapping on windows offering to sell you a parking space. Then there were those hateful little scooters weaving in and out of the gridlock, often mounting the pavements and trying to thread their way through the masses there.

The night also seemed to bring out more people than the day with many of the pavements so jammed it might be the end of a football match, a surging Manhattan mob all making their ways to . . . where? . . . where? . . . where are they all off to and, if it's so exciting, can I tag along? I actually fell in behind a couple walking in a business-like way only to find, about 20 minutes later, they had come back to the same spot and were still walking in a businesslike way.

But even as we all promenaded around, in our businesslike ways, I often thought of Dante and how he might even have been sitting over there, on a seat outside a *gelateria*, his beloved

Beatrice licking an ice cream next to him as, with a notebook on his knee, he looked around him and penned another few lines describing all these people desperately trying to crawl across the fiery, unforgiving plains of hell.

I had my own odd glimpse into hell the next day in the Piazza della Signoria when, while sitting with my notebook on my knee and trying to jot down a few thoughts, I looked up at the people crossing the square and saw, to my astonishment, they were falling over dead. *Bing, bong, bing.* They just came out of the alleyways with their handbags and plastic carriers when they fell down, face-first, on the same cobbles where Michelangelo had once walked and Savonarola had been burned. *Bing, bong, bing.* It was the middle of the morning too and I hadn't had a single drink.

But then, no sooner had my amazed eyelids given a few clearing winks, than I realized I had been hallucinating and that what I had been seeing in reality – or what I *thought* I had been seeing in reality – was what had often happened in my mind's eye while I had been out driving on the open road. And there it was again – *bing, bong, bing* – people falling dead on their faces and then – *bong, bing, bong* – all of them jumping up and walking on again.

This was just another version of what happened while I was driving – ideas staggering out and falling dead in front of me. But in a totally different way. So now my mind was mixing fact with fancy although there might be a sort of truth swirling around inside it all.

Our ideas organize and dictate almost everything we do. As the indivisible atoms of our thought processes they are central to our lives and culture. They tell us how we think about ourselves and form our views of the world. We *are* our ideas about ourselves. The world *adds up* to little more than our ideas about it. The most priceless gift a parent can give a child is the priceless gift of his good ideas. And already on this pilgrimage from Berlin to Rome we have been sniffing around the ideas of great men which both created and drove the Reformation and Renaissance.

Most of our actions also spring directly from our ideas and, if we receive our ideas from a systematic study of the Bible, say, the chances are we will act in a Christian way. If we take them from the modern cinema then we will surely act in a completely different way. Ideas have winged feet and the very best are ageless, durable angels which have flown down through the centuries while mere buildings have fallen into rubble and dust. The ideas of Jesus and St Paul have led to lasting revolutions in society and behaviour while those of such as Karl Marx, around which whole societies have been built, have quickly fallen and been found wanting.

So, given my ideas about ideas, perhaps my mind, here in the Piazza della Signoria, once the very centre of the Renaissance, was again underlining the importance of ideas by showing me a glimpse of people falling dead. Showing me, in a symbolic way, how the people looked up and were fed with the ideas of the great masters which, in time, set them free into a new dawn. Perhaps.

The real truth of it was I didn't really have a clue. I don't even regard myself as a philosopher if only because I haven't understood most of the philosophical works I have tackled. If I am anything at all, I am a reporter and all I ever really like to write about is what I see with my own two eyes. Who really knows the truth of anything except God?

Maybe what I saw was just a meaningless hallucination. Or maybe God, in a bored moment, was having one of his little jokes at my expense. He likes to do that from time to time – little puffs of wind on still days, a stern word in the mouth of a stranger or even the flash of an angel's wing – nothing very earth-shaking although he did once burst through to me in Malaya, full of raw fury, giving me my own vision of ideas, which left me shaking for weeks and even years and from which, even 40 years later, I still haven't recovered.

But if he was up to one of his little games again in Florence, I did so wish he would go and play around with someone else and told him so. My mind is the only one I've got and I don't like it being messed about like this. I also certainly don't want to feel the edge of his anger again until I drop.

Yet whatever really did happen to me in that square, when all those people were falling dead, it *was* a very strange moment and I *did* then go off and have a drink or three.

CHAPTER 9

Manic Street Preacher

I awoke on an old lake floor they call the Vale of Spoleto, peering out onto a landscape of misty ghosts moving about in the morning dew. There was a clear restlessness in these ghosts, sometimes opening up to reveal a glimpse of a ruined building or a line of cedars before closing ranks again and moving about some more, as if trying to decide among themselves what to reveal next. Already lots of birds were up and about singing the psalms of autumn.

This flat vale stretched for miles in every direction and, occasionally, an untidy jumble of red tiled roofs and a basilica scattered over a high hill, rose up out of the mists. This was the hill town of Assisi which seemed to float on those morning mists in the same improbable way that Venice floated on the sea. Dark mountains brooded in the distance like a bunch of anarchists discussing precisely where they were going to fling their next bomb.

Our cloudy views were then made cloudier by several fires that had been lit in a nearby field. The farmers may have been burning off the stubble but the black and grey smoke was billowing up thickly as if from small volcanoes. I could barely see anything at all although I did see the backsides of a few fleeing animals, on the run to another field perhaps which they hopefully weren't about to set on fire.

All at once about five figures, in corded habits, began taking shape in the mists, moving along the road in unclouded joy, making their way towards Assisi where, unless I was very much mistaken, they would beg from door to door, possessing nothing but the rags on their backs, before travelling on to the next place as pilgrims and strangers, defending the truth of their words with the simple beauty of their lives. You can always pick out those Franciscan fools for God. They are just a rabble of happiness really, come to taunt the emptiness of our own lives, come to briefly warm the coldness of our own hearts.

They disappeared into yet more mists and I made myself a cup of tea inside my camper, already knowing that today was going to be a fine day, perhaps even finer than the fine day I'd had the day before and the day before that.

The sun was soon shining hard and the mists lifted slightly. A lizard came out onto a rock before going back in again. I shaved in my wing mirror in which, just as I was working my way under my chin, I caught the briefest glimpse of him threading his way through a nearby vineyard. He might have been a farm labourer except he not so much walked as danced, a little like a butterfly collector leaping about in a meadow in hot pursuit of something extremely rare. There was that strange but somehow familiar laughter too. He was also being followed by a lamb and a pheasant.

You would know as soon as you looked at his nutty gait that you would fall in love with him. Here was a shout of joy on two legs, someone who was not only attractive to people in general and women particular but also someone whom even the animals found irresistible.

He cared desperately for all animals and birds, I was to learn, feeding the bees with honey and wine in the winter while also making nests for the doves. The only things he wasn't entirely mad about were ants whom he thought a little too frantic, always buzzing about the place and using up too much valuable energy getting nowhere. Yet what this prophet of the vineyards once said to the birds in the pulpit of this Umbrian countryside is said to be one of the greatest sermons ever delivered. Lean forward in your pews and listen awhile.

> My little sisters the birds you are much beholden to God your creator and you ought to praise him because he has given you the liberty to fly around in all places, and has given you double and triple raiment. And again you are beholden to him for the element of air which he has appointed for you, that you neither sow nor reap, but God feeds you and gives you the brooks and the fountains for you to drink, the mountains and valleys for your refuge and the tall trees wherein to make your nests. And since you know neither how to spin nor to stitch he clothes you and your loved ones. Wherefore your creator loves you much, since he has bestowed on you many benefits. And therefore take care, my little sisters, of the sin of ingratitude and study always to please God.

And that was his singing shadow in my wing mirror, dancing by in the mists, chasing an elusive butterfly and followed by his animals. We may have met him before. We may have heard his Mekon laughter once before.

The sun had finally swept the mists out of the streets of Assisi and I was puffing and sweating a fair bit as I climbed her steeply rising streets. The first of the tourist buses was pulling into the large car park down below and my mouth kept picking up the tastes of baking bread and roasting coffee. Vendors had opened their souvenir shops and were sitting in their doorways sullenly. There were surely too many of them, packed cheek by jowl, hawking row upon row and pile upon pile of useless plastic memorabilia.

All around the great Basilica it was like a Berlin building site. Drills were drilling and jackhammers pounding. They were still repairing the place after an earthquake shook it to its foundations a few years back, killing four people and the local pilgrim trade. You can still pick out lots of cracks in the walls and paving stones almost everywhere you look.

This Basilica is, in fact, three piled into one: the crypt which contains his sarcophagus, the Middle Church, as large as a cathedral, where they have restored the frescoes and the collapsed roof, and the equally large Upper Church which, today, was still closed for repairs.

Inside they were still busy recreating a key medieval painting of St Matthew by Cimabue. The problem was that it had come crashing down in 120,000 fragments in the earthquake. But they have since scanned all the fragments into a computer with the help of IBM. The computer can recognize a match between two colours and even the continuity of individual brush strokes. Somehow it can match one tiny fragment with the other and, any day now, Matthew was going to come together in this giant jigsaw and return to his rightful place on the Upper Church.

Yet despite all the hammering and dust this place did have a serious and spiritual atmosphere which is rare in places overrun by tourists and the sound of jackhammers. You just knew you could put in some serious prayer here as you wandered the darkened nave with polished stone floors. Brilliant frescoes roamed the walls and ceilings: every contemporary painter of note once worked here, all paying tribute to the Poor Little Man – Il Poverello – after he died.

I came across a row of polished confessional boxes where, in the light of one and through the wooden lattice, I could just about make out the bowed head of a grey-haired priest waiting patiently to listen to the next episode of the never-ending soap opera of modern sin. Would he today hear anything new? Would someone tell him something which would briefly rouse his interest? Could anyone possibly ever come up with a new variation on the same old story? I doubted it and one of the few times I am really glad I'm not a priest is when I see one sitting in a confessional, head bowed and bracing himself for the worst. Who could possibly want to listen to *that* all day?

The Basilica didn't even charge for admission, which was something of a refreshing change in this part of the world and even the priest on a desk to take offerings seemed more interested in reading the Bible than hitting the visitors with mugging smiles. NO GUIDED TOURS, said a sign. *SILENZIO.*

In one of the chapels, put aside for private prayer, an old lady was giving her all, actually lifting her eyes to the altar and speaking her pleas out loud, when the priest on the Offerings desk abandoned his Bible and stooped down next to her listening to what she was saying. I'm not at all sure that priests are supposed to interfere in prayers like this but there he was, whispering into her ear as she continued to ignore him and directly address the altar. He stood up only to bend down for another few words and then left her to it. It is always mildly thrilling watching priests shepherding their flocks in an age when so many have given up or lock themselves away out of sight.

Francis was born here in 1182, the son of Pietro Bernardone, a rich businessman and his wife Pica, a native of Provence. He attached little importance to his studies and concentrated on business matters in the episcopal school in Assisi. He learned to read and write from a primer composed mainly of prayers in the vernacular and psalms in Latin. They were also taught some grammar and rhetoric but he was not a good student, anxious to become a successful businessman like his father.

Umbria was a place of many warring tribes at the time and soon after leaving school Francis fought with the Assisian cavalry against their ancient rivals Perugia. In one battle they were badly beaten and Francis was taken prisoner and flung into a gaol in Perugia.

Soon, however, he was out again and working in his father's shop in Assisi which sold silk, velvet, brocade and satin. He also became something of a playboy, forever flinging his money around 'as though he were the son of a prince' to the extent that he was actually reprimanded by the Bishop of Assisi for blowing his father's fortune. He was soon to feel the need to escape from the town's soulless pleasure-seeking and a sudden illness brought him face to face with a solitude deep within him. He even toyed with the idea of becoming a knight but, on the eve of setting off for a crusade, an impoverished nobleman said he could not afford a suit of armour and, on impulse, Francis gave him his. Francis had found a new inner voice and the pattern of his life was set.

In the tiny church of St Damian in Assisi he prostrated himself before a painting of Christ when the image began talking to him. The image spoke to him by name and said: 'Go, Francis and repair my house because it is falling into ruin.'

From that moment on Francis was possessed by the fire and certainty of his vision. It never let him go in a life which was profoundly radical and dynamically creative. There *must* have been times when he roundly cursed that vision and wanted to lay it down. But you can never lay a vision down because you have become tired of it. Visions are tenacious and can possess all your waking hours. Once seen, they nag and torment and refuse to let you be. They hold you in the firm grip of their truth even when your body is torn by faithlessness and guilt. Even when you are lying in the gutter, in a pool of blood and vomit, listening to the cracked siren calls of alcoholism, you will still be possessed by your vision. Even when your thoughts become as a sewer and your resolve has been broken on the anvil of sexual lust, a vision from God will stay with you, often as brightly and clearly as that first appalling moment of lucidity when it was delivered. Visions actually derange you although you must keep speaking their truth even when your friends clearly believe you have become as mad as a box.

Duly enslaved by his vision, Francis stripped himself of all his possessions and gave them to the poor. But he did keep spending his father's money to build churches and was duly taken to court by his father. Outside the courtroom he vented his anger at his profligate son in a loud and irate voice. Francis only replied with one of the theatrical gestures for which he was later to become famous. He took off all his clothes and threw them at his father's feet. He now had nothing whatsoever and remained in that blessed state for almost all his life.

From that moment he wandered the countryside, meditated in caves and performed acts of penance. He lived as a hermit and begged alms before coming back to Assisi, with only the rags on his back, where he went around asking for lime and stones so that he could rebuild the church at St Damian.

He also became the original manic street preacher, standing on any available box or wall to proclaim his message – not one of Christ, the glittering king on a throne of gold but that of a bloody and suffering Christ with torn hands and a breaking heart. This message was delivered in simple words and could be understood immediately by ordinary folk. He also believed in introducing the odd *coup de théâtre* as he spoke, once telling the people of Assisi to stay right where they were before going into the Church of San Rufino, taking off all his clothes and asking one of his followers to 'drag him naked in front of the people with the cord of his habit tied around his neck'. He also told his followers to fill a bowl with ashes, climb onto the platform where he had been preaching and empty the ashes onto his head. With such visual aids, he believed, we would come closer to God and be better able to understand – and enter into – the sufferings of Christ himself.

He also wanted the people to know what the actual birth of Christ was like. Not an absurdly heavenly business, decked out with glittering angels and shafts of golden light, but a messy, even dirty business on the floor of a stable. To this end he conceived a vivid tableau of the Nativity complete with life-like models of Joseph, Mary and Christ. This was the first crib scene and he wanted it to emphasize Christ's poverty and vulnerability. This emphasis would later be taken up by the Catholic Church and launch the world of art into a new period of realistic naturalism. Almost single-handedly Francis brought Christ down to earth.

His didactic purpose was always to inspire a faith of *feeling* rather than reason. We could enter into the mysteries through our emotions. His religion was feeling, Henry Thode wrote in 1885. The preaching in which he revealed it worked through feeling; his relation to men and nature was conditioned by feeling. Therein lay the explanation of his powerful influence.

Later that morning in the great Basilica in Assisi I came across a museum with lots of his relics. The Church of the Relics of St Francis, it said outside in 13 languages. His habit, set out in one large glass case, actually made me laugh out loud since it was a scabby old thing which wouldn't have got through an Oxfam shop door on a slow week, patched with this and that, moth-eaten and full of holes. His sandals were also on view, which could have been donated to him by a Bombay beggar although there was a nice, white tunic which could have been his pyjamas.

After leaving the museum I finally found a small crypt where a service was going on in front of a simple stone sarcophagus containing his remains and guarded by a few vases of fresh lilies and a wrought-iron gate. A group of pilgrims was singing heartily, accompanied by a lively guitar and, as they continued their joyful song, I knelt and stared at that rough stone sarcophagus and I thought of Francis and my own visions which had also imprisoned me for more than 30 years now.

I thought of the time when God broke through to me in

Malaya; those days of bedlam and visions which are never really far from my mind, although they seemed particularly vivid this morning, kneeling here in front of the tomb of St Francis, the great visionary himself.

After I graduated from University College Cardiff I went to South-East Asia, the first graduate to go to Indonesia with Voluntary Service Overseas, only to be thrown out of Djakarta after a few months because of President Sukarno's confrontation with the 'neo-colonialist plot' of Malaysia. A short time in Singapore followed and then I was sent to the Sultan Abdul Hamid College in Alor Star, North Malaya, where I was to teach English. This was a small, scrappy town surrounded by rice fields and just near the Thai border. With little to do on weekends and in the evenings after I'd finished teaching I mostly stayed in my hut where I lived with my pet mynah bird and worked on my great novel.

The book was a rambling, undisciplined affair about the often violent struggle of three men to come to terms with themselves and one another. With less than a month to go before my time was up, I had written well over four hundred pages with the struggle between my protagonists intense, if not murderous, and no resolution in sight.

The narrative was set in a small Malayan town like Alor Star and explored the relationship between a young teacher and a broken old commodities broker which was gradually being destroyed and overtaken by the cold calculations of a homosexual rubber planter who was given to periodic bouts of awesome violence. My themes were alienation, violence and arcane sexuality.

The important point about the book, though, was not its haphazard narrative but that, in the spirit of much contemporary work, it was romantic, a school with which I was becoming increasingly familiar at the time since I was teaching the 'classical' T. S. Eliot. By romantic I mean someone with a persistent attraction to the violent, the perverted, the melancholy and the cruel. The romantic is also obsessed by sexual inconstancy, arguing that the law of the individual is above all other laws. A romantic will strike an attitude and ignore all that contradicts it. He exalts the imagination over the rule of reason and will always argue for the triumph of impulse over order.

His key stance is that he will unfailingly ignore the claims of the real world and ordinary people in his work and, in his determined pursuit of such bizarre preoccupations as murder, drugs, astrology, perversion and the occult reveal himself to be totally lost and unable to stumble out of the fog of romanticism.

Early one evening I was sitting on the edge of my bed looking over at the manuscript when its pages juddered slightly as if electrified. I blinked a lot and continued looking but it was just a pile of papers. I later decided that what I would do was kill off all the characters to finish the book, but despite some bouts of lurid violence, they always seemed to survive. One night, about a week later, someone did die though. My mynah bird.

I had built it a perch just above my typewriter and noticed that a blue film had formed over its eyes with its whole body listing slightly and its wings shivering. Yet, just when it appeared that the bird was going to topple forward off its perch, it righted itself again, its eyes opening to reveal the thick blue film which was completely covering its pupils. I picked up my jar of recently caught grasshoppers, which the bird normally snaffled up greedily, but it turned away and its body listed forward again. Those big, blue eyes of death opened wide.

I walked back to my bed. My mind was elsewhere. I had driven it deep into a cul-de-sac and the brick walls all around were high and unscaleable. I lit a cigarette and giggled a bit as I sucked it down. Later I tried blowing smoke rings but the fan kept breaking up the barely formed wisps. An hour later the bird plummeted off its perch and landed with a soft thud on its back on the floor.

The very sound of the thud made my heart jump and, with a wave of grief breaking over me, I walked over to it and went down on my knees to touch it. The breeze of the fan ruffled its feathers and I even seemed to be able to hear the footsteps of the small lizards who went rushing around on the ceiling above. The noise of two moths flying around the light was as loud as that of two bats.

I sat down at my desk and rolled a sheet of paper into my typewriter but no sooner had I lifted my hands than I let them fall again. There was a rustle in the sheaf of papers that was my novel and the sound scared me so much I jumped back and knocked over the chair which made a resounding crack on the floor. I was scared of what was going to happen because something *was* going to happen. That much was clear.

I lit another cigarette and pulled my fingertips across my eyes feeling very weary indeed. When I looked at my book again I saw a fungus ball growing out of it. It was one of the most amazing things I have ever seen. It just swelled and swelled remorselessly until it completely covered the lower half of the window. The ball glowed with a startlingly brilliant light and it seemed to be made out of translucent jelly with red, orange and purple veins running out of its heart and circling back into it. Ideas were trickling along the veins like tadpoles, falling down to feed on the small, dark heart before swimming back up the veins again. Sometimes a viscous, fast-running idea shot along a vein and hurtled back into the heart, causing the fungus to vibrate and slightly change its shape. Faces moved around in it too, rising up like fish and turning to smile before fading back into the heart. I studied it for a long time in silence and sniffed.

This giant fungus, I knew without having to be told, represented the poisoned and poisoning growth of my own romanticism; the dead and ugly vision which brings nothing but death and despair to the world. I did not understand why I knew this so clearly and certainly. I just did. I tried to stand up but my legs would not let me. I tried to turn around but my body was frozen. The glowering fungus just hung there burning into my consciousness for perhaps an hour, or two, or three – or it might have been five minutes – when, as slowly as it had grown, it shivered into nothing and, in a blast of warm air, the room went black. My body, released, collapsed back onto the bed.

I was lying there twitching a bit when I felt fluttering movements around my arms, legs and chest. I sat up and gazed at the wall. It was no longer dark but nothing made sense. The feeling was of my face smashed up against a mirror. The face had broken into a fragmented image with the different parts of the mirror reflecting, in a hundred different ways, the numerous images of the same face. I tried to focus on the wall but the galvanized forces of something were now in overdrive. I stood up, turned and caught sight of my manuscript when something hot and quick darted down inside me and the ideas of the book rose up out of it, swept through my mind and rushed around the room like a swarm of angry bees.

They massed in one top corner of the room, buzzing and swelling, then swept down through my brain again. It was a bit like staring down a well with a furious gale blowing up out of it and I was forced to hold the top of my head tightly lest it should be blown off. The ideas leaked out of every part of my body; through my fingers, ears and eyes; pouring down through my cheeks and over my chest. I tried to punch my unravelling head back into shape but only hit a sparkling, dancing jumble of nonsensical ideas reaching up out of books and films and plays . . . all travelling through – and smashing against one another in – my body where, deep down, yet more ideas were being generated which, in turn, whipped up the swirling tides into great tempests of ideas. The romantic meets his blitz. My own dogs had finally got me. Oh God, please call off the dogs.

He did not call them off but sent in further packs the next week when, only occasionally aware of myself as an individual, I kept stumbling around the town, lost to myself and my work, while seeing the most fearful visions. My pupils often found me standing alone or wandering somewhere near the outskirts of the town.

One night I stumbled down to the river bank, my brain swelling and contracting like an overworked lung, my hands pressing down hard on the top of my skull, fearful that my brain was going to burst. I lay down on the bank with my arms around my head and had a vision of the world.

I saw a silvery plain with hundreds, perhaps thousands of small matchstick people milling around on it. Tiny ideas were flitting between their heads in looping arcs and lightning dashes. A cliff was overhanging this plain and, all along the edge, demonic bands of artists were loosing off volleys of wild, fizzing ideas which were shelling the people below. As the volleys became wilder and more intense the movements of the matchstick people on the plain became more and more agitated and they were rioting, jumping on one another and rolling around, fighting among themselves. The ideas of all those on the cliff-edge were *romantic* and, just lying there gazing at this extraordinary vision, I saw that the world was but a rising, multiplying jungle of ideas in which the artists were corrupt and the people corrupted.

I rolled over onto my side and vomited. Later, still immobilized by the shock of what I had seen, I was found staring up at the night by two of my pupils. They took me back to my room and I felt as if half of my brain had been shot away, just looking around me with my hands clamped firmly on my head like a prisoner of war.

The next time I became aware of myself again I was walking along one of the town's back streets when the silvery plain came back except that, this time, it was me who was standing on the cliff-edge with destructive ideas shooting out of my mouth and rocketing the people below. This time my ideas were like conkers on vast lengths of string whirling down out of my mind before whirling back again. So I, too, was as corrupt as the rest of them, I was told, and I cried out because I thought my head was about to explode.

I have never understood how I got through the next few weeks since, long after discovering that my ideas were irresponsibly destructive, I continued brainstorming, choking and getting lost. One afternoon while walking along the main street and trying to get home it all seemed beyond me since, no sooner had I decided where my hut was and tried to stumble towards it, than I saw another part of my past or a book I had read or a film which had affected my behaviour. It was a great shock seeing that I was but the construct of other people. Then, while pondering on this, I would stumble past my hut and end up on the other side of town.

A brief and final vision came one weekend, in Penang. I was sitting looking up at a clear, blue sky when it looked as if it was bleeding with black blood. Then a hole appeared with a series of golden revolving drums moving around one another inside it. A shower of fat black ideas came streaming out of that hole. The black rain.

The night before I left Malaya I was lying on my bed with my brain simmering and running when I felt a warm, breathing presence within and all around me. This presence moved closer and deeper into me and I abandoned myself to it. Tears bubbled out of my closed eyes and I opened my arms wide feeling so warm, secure and trusting that nothing, in that moment, could have caused me any fear. The palm of a hand smoothed my smashed brain which bubbled and moved around with its soothing presence. The presence became even more deeper and loving and I lifted my head to try and see it when it lifted out of my body, leaving me there on the bed, alone.

I knew then that God had bashed me up good but had at least had the grace to come back briefly to offer his apologies.

In a sense all my subsequent life has been a search for an understanding of those visions. I have written about them often and have never once thought that they didn't come directly from God; never doubted that, in those few, fiery weeks, he showed me his world just as he sees it. Those visions are never far from my mind or heart if only because they also represent the moment of my complete conversion.

In Malaya I came face to face with a truth from which I have never really recovered. Every new year has brought a fresher and deeper understanding of the truth of those visions; and I believe that the romantic ideas and philosophies of our film-makers, painters and writers – with their persistent pursuits of the violent, the perverted, the melancholy and the cruel – *are* actively destroying this world and our faith in God. The fungus has become our real modern icon and all of us are dying in this long and terrifying season of black rain.

And so it was that, kneeling in front of the tomb of St Francis, with my mind running through the detail and circumstances of those appalling visions yet again, I felt close to the old saint and the way he must have suffered a lot. I was even sure I heard a peal of Mekon laughter coming from somewhere since I was not surprised to discover that I was also kneeling there with my hands on the top of my head like some captured prisoner of war. I often find myself doing this since it seems to ease the pain in my brain as it swells up against the roof of my skull whenever I think of those wild and whirling moments as I was bounced around inside the anxieties of God himself.

But why me? Why did you have to go and pick on me?

I picked my way through the fields and vineyards of the Vale of Spoleto the next morning, following the distant, high dome of the Basilica of St Mary of the Angels which is so big and central to the plain it actually seemed to be pinioning it down.

The earthquake didn't spare this Basilica either – even shaking the gilded angel off the roof – and there was still a lot of work going on inside. But it did contain a real surprise since, right in the middle of it, was a small, stone chapel, sitting there oddly like a Christmas grotto in a department store. Apparently this was the chapel where Francis had lived and first founded his order, making his home near a leper colony for which he cared so much. A whole flock of bird-like nuns in brown habits – who may have been Tamils – were kneeling in prayer inside the chapel and, just nearby, was another small stone chapel, with bars on the door and money scattered over the floor, where Francis had died. (There are a number of mysteries in my life I will never understand: why people buy rap records, why Ken Morse is always on rostrum camera and why toast always falls buttered side down. Here were a couple more: why do they take a perfectly nice chapel and overwhelm it by a church almost the size of St Peter's in Rome in memory of a man who specifically ordered his followers not to build fine churches? And why had they scattered money over the floor where he had died when not only did Francis never want any money but always refused to even touch the stuff?)

This was the tiny chapel of Porziuncola, I was to discover, so-called because of the tiny parcel of land on which it was built. It was at a morning Mass here that Francis was told that 'the disciples of Christ must possess neither gold nor silver nor money, nor any wallets or purse, nor a staff on the road. Nor must they have footwear, not two tunics but preach only the kingdom of God and repentance.' He was captured immediately by these notions. 'This is what I want, this is what I ask and this is what I yearn to do with all my heart.' And he threw away the few things he had left. Materialism would be subordinated to the spirit.

Soon he took a group of followers – the Penitents of Assisi – to Rome to meet the Pope. We still have reports of a 'short, thin young man with burning eyes' with bare feet and a penitential look on his face. This man asked for papal sanction to live in penitential poverty and, so the story goes, the Pope was initially reluctant but had a dream that night. He had seen the Lantern Basilica about to fall down when a young man ran to prop it up with his shoulders. The Pope saw this young man was indeed Francis and so began the Franciscan Order. The Order then lived here on the Spoleto Vale in abject poverty. They often went without bread, content to beg for scraps even if they never 'complained or grumbled and patiently endured all with a lightness of heart and gladness of spirit'.

He wondered what was perfect joy. Well, he thought, it might be returning from Perugia on a freezing, winter night to his small chapel here in Porziuncola. The mud had formed into icicles on his tunic which had drawn blood on his legs. After knocking for a long time a friar came, denounced him as a simpleton and told him to go away. 'And if I endure all this patiently and without dismay I say to you, therefore, that therein lies perfect joy.'

These ragamuffins possessed nothing except the rags on their backs and even not them. That ragged tunic belonging to Francis I had seen earlier in Assisi wasn't his either it seems. The warden who had given it to him had said: 'Put on this tunic for holy obedience, which I am merely lending you. And so that you may be sure you have no property rights with regard to it, I forbid you to give it others.'

Even this tiny chapel, which became the centre of the Order, didn't belong to them. Every year Francis and his followers paid the Abbot of Mount Subasio with a basket of fish as a symbolic rent. Francis said that friars must not possess house, nor land nor anything else whatsoever. They are to pass through this world as pilgrims and strangers, seeing the Lord in poverty and humility and begging for alms with confidence and without shame. 'Let poverty be your party.'

'May God give you peace,' the friars called out wherever they walked, often dissolving division and local hatreds by their mere presence. Within ten years they numbered 3,000 and Francis preached to one man with as much care and attention as he might devote to a huge crowd. But sometimes mere words failed this dramatic man of thunder and dew to the extent that he might just give them all his blessing and then walk away.

We have one reasonably good description of him at this time from his first biographer Tommaso da Celano who had also met him.

> He was a man who spoke freely, of joyous aspect with a benevolent countenance far removed from softness or haughtiness; of average height, indeed rather short; a rotund, not very large head; elongated, thin body; forehead smooth, not broad; medium-size black eyes; ingenious look; dark hair; straight eyebrows; nose, thin and regular; ears prominent but small; smooth temples; tongue without venom; a voice full of fervour and passion, penetrating, clear, sorrowful; even, white, strong teeth; small, thin lips; black, unkempt beard; slender neck; straight shoulders; fine hands with long fingers tapering into well-modelled nails; spindly legs; small feet; delicate skin; a minimum of flesh. He dressed in a tunic of coarse fabric, hardly ever slept and his hand was ever an open act of generosity.

In the final years of his ministry he became embroiled in many savage polemics, largely about how his Order should develop, so he withdrew more and more into solitude and the mystical contemplation of the Godhead. By the age of 42, 'this little madman in the world' was worn out by penitence and illness and sought out lonely caves in surrounding mountains. Here, in these caves, he spoke with God even, at one point, asking the birds to refrain from singing while he said his prayers.

He had a mystical communion with almost all of nature. If they were creatures of God, they were his brothers and sisters. The flowers, grass and bees were all brothers and sisters. No plant could be cut. No insect could be harmed. Even dousing a fire was a crime. 'No brother, don't harm the fire.' When his eyes were being cauterized by a red-hot poker, in some doomed attempt to restore his failing eyesight, he said: 'Be careful with me Brother Fire, because I have always loved you.'

The final seal on his great life came when three of his followers took him up Mount Verna where they stayed in a wooden hut. Francis went out alone and, while meditating, flames danced around his head and he saw a vision of flaming angels and Christ crucified. Then, as the vision lifted, his own hands felt the sharp, angry blows of the nails. Blood flowed from his hands and the right side of his body as if pierced by a lance. He had been given the Stigmata and he was to bleed like this, much to his eternal pain and embarrassment, right up to his death. Yes, Brother Body had finally brought him to the end of his magical, mystical road.

Death came and ground him down slowly, as death does – unless you are lucky enough to be run down by a big, red bus or stop an accurate bullet. He first lost his sight and then the use of his legs. His stomach and feet had also swollen up before he was taken back to the security of the hill fort at Assisi because they were fearful his body might be stolen by Perugia. But he insisted on being brought back here to his beloved chapel, to this very spot in Portziuncola 'so that the life of the body should end where the life of the soul had begun'.

Even in his most desperate illness he composed his Canticle of the Creatures here, now considered one of the greatest jewels in the crown of Italian poetry. This song would end his life, he knew, and his followers still sing it in public after sermons 'in order to lift the hearts of men and lead them to God in gladness and pain'. All he ever asked for, to relieve his pain, was a little marzipan or parsley.

As he was dying he greeted his beloved Lady Poverty and asked that he be stripped naked and covered with ashes. Then, on 3 October 1226, on that very spot where all those Tamil nuns are still deep in prayer, he uttered a line from a Psalm; 'Free my soul from prison, so that I may praise thy name' and, with a flight of larks rising up from the roof, he died.

There was a service on the main altar that morning and I was about to leave when I realized it was being conducted in English. I was also familiar with about every step of the service, which was a bit unusual around these parts, so I sat down to listen to what the officiating priest had to say:

> St Francis was a poor man. His poverty is another highlight of the same poverty as that shown by Mary. It gives us the possibility of escaping from greed. Poverty also enables us to find time for God who flows into our hearts like the oil from the Mount of Olives. And so like Christ. But the cost is always the Cross, participating in the suffering of Christ. St Francis shows us union with Christ, particularly with the Stigmata. Through the gift of faith we become members of the church of the body of Christ.

Still puzzled by this unexpected outbreak of Englishness I approached him after the service and learned that he was a Catholic priest from Westminster in London, Father Michael Roberts, over here with a travel group called SPES and leading a 39-strong party on a pilgrimage to Rome. He invited me along to lunch with them at a nearby restaurant where I also shared a table with another Christian and his wife, both Chinese, now living in Walsall but originally from Ipoh in North Malaya. (Ah, Malaya again! When will I ever come to avoid it?) We all agreed to meet up in Rome later that week.

That night, with a blood-red crescent moon pinned up against the Umbrian sky, I walked around the Vale of Spoleto and came across Francis again. Frogs burped and crickets erupted together suddenly like banks of mobile phones and his spirit was right there, I knew, still moving through the vineyards and destined to haunt this land forever. Cars accelerated past and I caught his outline in the whirling headlamps, standing there, laughing madly as he spoke about the freedom of poverty or the need for penance or the order that we should all love our neighbour.

Since his death he has become the all-time champion of the underdog, be it the hunted fox or the dancing bear. He has taught us that we should always look after our sacred world, especially our water and rivers. Nothing was beyond the reach of his radical care and it was interesting, I thought, that the Catholic Church made him a saint just two years after his death – faster than anyone before him or since.

But being out here on this plain for the last few days and always able to lift my pilgrim eyes to the distant hill of Assisi, had helped me too. Francis' story had told me something about God's forcefulness and unwillingness to let go; it had again told me that the Path of the Cross was always difficult, often full of gladness and pain, but pretty much paved with suffering and despair too. You really never do know what's going to happen to you when you take this path.

Francis' story had also told me that you just do not give in to drink and drugs after God has knocked you around a bit.

You should just get up, dust yourself down and get on with it. But, yes, the path is hard and tough and, when you think you can't take it any more, it just gets harder and tougher.

Men like Luther, Galileo and Francis become as lanterns as we pick our way through the darkness along this path. We take their light and try to add them to our own light. Knowledge of their lives and the manner and place where they lived them adds to, and deepens, our own spirituality. They enable us to see ahead better and with more courage. This is what happens to you when you go on a pilgrimage.

I was also seeing that this journey was yet again giving me a deeper understanding of – and better perspective on – my own visions. I was coming to see the way they always cling to you, no matter how hard you try and shake them off or put them down. When they are given to you they are yours for life. You can make them your armour or they'll turn into your ball and chain. Either way there is no getting rid of them.

And even in this inspiring, cricket-whirring night, here with Francis in Umbria, being watched only by a blood-red crescent moon, I could still see the eternal truth of my own visions. I could do this merely by walking down the road and peering into the living rooms of homes where families were gathered around their televisions; homes where they were watching an endless procession of bullets, perversions, cruelty, death and violence; homes which were awash with the polluted waters of the black rain.

Hannibal Lecter has become the great icon of modern evil and there he was on that screen, before me now, making strange noises behind that glass prison. And he was portrayed by a Welshman like me too. A Welshman like me!

So, one way or another, there was much for my notebook that night with Francis on the Vale of Spoleto. Notes on the pure radiance of the past and the polluted darkness of the present. Notes on my own failings and weaknesses and notes on others' strengths and successes. Oh aye. Notes on the whole damn thing before setting out on the last leg of my autumnal pilgrimage – down the main *autostrada* to Rome.

CHAPTER 10

The Majesty that is Rome

It was yet another *buongiorno* morning and we were gathered on a subway platform in the station of Prima Porta, a rather seedy, haphazard town at the end of the line and directly north of Rome. Rather than do battle with the traffic, in streets where they all seem to still think they are racing chariots, I had decided to camp on a site with the marvellously inspiring name of Happy Camper and commute into the city daily along with the rest of the Roman *popolino*.

The carriages of these subway trains were almost completely swathed in graffiti in the Manhattan style. Blue, green and red swirls of aerosolled nothingness enlivened by the occasional word, detached eyeball or swastika. Mostly they seemed to be the signatures of illiterate Leonardos although, if their styles were unruly, it was as nothing compared to the scramble for seats when the carriage doors opened. A queue is not a queue as we normally understand it in the Eternal City; it is something to do with starting blocks and sharp elbows; a concept which you negotiate with aggression and speed. Here queues are purely advisory, which you try to sweep aside as best you can. You certainly do not *join* the back of the thing.

But you do soon get the hang of making your way through the scrum and, more by luck than judgement, my behind actually managed to fall down into an empty seat next to a young woman who was reading a paperback. The rest in the carriage were such as you might find travelling to work in any

European city: a young girl absent-mindedly picking her zits, a man opposite talking to himself, several reading newspapers and a youth with a baseball cap on back to front trying, but failing, to make a call on a mobile phone.

I'd got on my best clothes, which is to say everything in my camper which wasn't dirty, since I was on my way to an audience with the Pope.

A burst of accordion music lit up the other end of the carriage and a dirty hand rattled a plastic Coca-Cola cup, with a few coins in it, under my nose. This was the first of the beggars which turned out to be a more or less constant procession all day, particularly when you ride the subway, most of them getting off the train at one station and crossing the platform to get on another. There were wandering mandolin and accordion players, singers of melancholy songs about abandoned homelands, gypsy hustlers, young girls with babies in shawls and any number of old men and women with severed or broken limbs which they waved at you plaintively.

You could always try to ignore them with a stony-faced coldness but I quickly learned that it was far easier for everyone concerned to keep a pocketful of small change and use a couple of coins to ease them on over to their next customer. Not that begging was so bad in Rome. We might remember that St Francis also made the pilgrimage to Rome and, so the story goes, was so appalled by the paucity of pilgrim offerings in St Peter's he threw all his money down on the floor and ended up flat broke on the streets, exchanging his clothes for a beggar's and spending the rest of the day begging for food 'with an unaccustomed joy of spirit'.

I suppose I should have tried this too, which might well have given me, if not an unaccustomed joy of spirit, then a little light comedy for this book. Perhaps I could have freshened up my chest operation scar with some bright lipstick, borrowed a crutch or two and tried manipulating the tourists around the Colosseum by looking close to death. Maybe even make a bit of money while I was at it. But, quite simply, I didn't have the bottle for it.

As the terminus at Flaminio approached, the young woman next to me put away her paperback into her handbag and took out a photograph album whereupon she began carefully scrutinizing the fuzzy snaps of a few children in bathing costumes playing with a ball on a beach. Presumably they were *her* children and, as she turned over the pages, she occasionally let out a long sigh of something which may well have been maternally wistful.

Italian women seem to adore their children with an unreal intensity and here it was again. All in all it can't be a barrel of laughs being a baby in Latin parts since, as soon as you make an appearance in the street in your pram, that is the signal for women of all ages to come scooting out from wherever and start dribbling over you or pinching your cheeks or twisting your big toe around in directions it wasn't designed to go. This is why most of them have dummies jammed in their mouths – to calm the little mutts down and stop them crying after having their big toes pulled every which way.

I changed trains at Flaminio and stewed in another soup of garlic breath, body odour and plaintive penury until we came to Ottaxiano station which was just next to St Peter's Square where I had my date with the Pope. But here again I took the wrong turning before meeting up with two American brothers, Michael and Brian Schumacher, who were both in Rome on holiday. We consulted a street map and then all took off to meet the Pope in the Square.

It might be the easiest ever prosecution under the Trade Description Act to say I was on my way for an audience with the Pope since this was Wednesday morning and there were about 50,000 other pilgrims jammed in the square and waiting for his holiness to make an appearance. Newspapers often talk of half a million pilgrims packing into this square but most of them have long abandoned straight news for eccentric fiction – particularly the Italian papers. They even talk of a million pilgrims in here at Easter but that is again impossible, particularly when you consider there are only 50,000 hotel beds in Rome and just a further 20,000 in pilgrim hostels.

A choir was singing as the rather opulent Swiss Guards stood around in their red, yellow and blue uniforms with their big, black floppy hats and white ruffs. Cardinals and bishops were mingling underneath a large canopy at the entrance to the church and quite a few were also up there in wheelchairs. This must be one of the times when it is actually good to be in a wheelchair since not only do you get the best seat right in the centre of the action, you also get to shake hands with the Pope.

I have been to one of these Wednesday morning audiences with the Pope once before, on another short pilgrimage to Rome, and a very cheerful time it was. Groups are often given completely spurious titles to get in there and our travel company had designated us, falsely, as all coming from the Church of the Sacred Heart in Blackpool. What had happened on that morning was that the Pope came out onto the stage and, in a variety of languages, told us all about his recent holidays in the Gambia. Then various groups were introduced to him. A group from the Italian army stood up and sang *Oh my Papa*. An American choir sang him their college song and, when the pilgrims from the Church of the Sacred Heart, Blackpool were introduced, we all duly stood up and sheepishly waved our handkerchiefs as he waved wanly back.

But today I was but another pilgrim to Rome in a sea of thousands, listening to an organ playing *Ave Maria*. Then, for no apparent reason, everyone began standing up as hands were waving and the applause became louder. We were at the back of the crowd and couldn't see what was going on when, as if by some tricky illusion, the familiar shape of John Paul II seemed to begin rising up over everyone's heads, almost as if he was water-skiing over a sea of waving hands and flags, until you could see that he was actually standing in his little jeep, being flanked and followed by many police.

Now aged 79, with Parkinson's, he looked much older and frailer than I remembered but there was still that old smiling warmth and, with all the joyous shouts and spontaneous bursts of applause, you picked up on the widening pools of emotion in the parting pilgrim throngs all around him. This is a man who is much loved and, even as a semi-hardline evangelical Protestant, I have never had any problems with him any more than I've had immersing myself in a Catholic service, often finding so few points of difference, even in the words, I've never quite been able to understand what all the fuss was about. Martin Luther and St Francis can only have been the different sides of the same coin, the one reacting to the corruption of his times and the other shining a new light on the darkness of his. I wouldn't have minded being in a foxhole with either of them. Or indeed this Pope who has always struck me as being the very pinnacle of geniality.

He smiled and we smiled. He smiled back and waved and we smiled and waved back. The morning was but a carnival of smiles when he was around and it was good to be a Christian here in Rome.

And for all our frequent Protestant chest-beating we also forget that the Celtic Church actually grew out of the Mother Church here in Rome. The Celtic Church, from the earliest period, not only believed in the Mass, the Sacraments and the other doctrines of the Catholic Church but was also in communion with the See of Rome. Also every Celtic saint worth his salt made a pilgrimage to Rome and even the great Welsh lawgiver Howel Dda was not satisfied with the laws he had drawn up until they had been sent to Rome and given the Pope's approval.

But that was all then and this is now, with the Pope taking up his throne, beneath the canopy and huge façade of St Peter's Church, where he spoke for about ten minutes in slow and slurred words which were often unintelligible. He coughed a lot too and finished with a *Grazi*.

Even so it was all you could really hope for here at the end of a long pilgrimage through central Europe, sitting at his feet in a crowded, sun-dappled square with the pigeons flapping about overhead. Lovely breezes played around the surrounding colonnades and again the words of a cardinal on the microphone underlined the universality of the Catholic Church. 'Most holy Father the English pilgrims are glad to bring you their respect and esteem,' he said. 'You are assured of their prayers. We also have a group of students and teachers from Denmark. We have a group from a university in Japan and other groups from Chicago, Ohio and Detroit. I also extend a particular welcome to the Lutheran groups from Latvia.'

The audience ended with the Pope giving everyone his apostolic blessing and then meeting his cardinals and those in wheelchairs. The rest of us drifted back from where we had come: doing battle with the comings and goings in the streets of Rome. And this long, hot season without end. You sensed that everyone had had enough of the sun by now. They'd had a hot summer followed by an even hotter autumn. Now forever puffing and blowing and fanning themselves they wanted some rain – or even a little snow perhaps – something to cool them down.

—

There is a dark and not entirely pleasant side to the Rome pilgrimage, I was to discover, in the form of its increasing commercialization. Rome's main source of income is from pilgrims and the Vatican has long been kept going by pilgrim money. At the time of my visit it was busy cashing in on the forthcoming Millennium celebrations, selling £25 Millennium Kits with a medallion and a special papal prayer with your name or family name which 'you will receive in one day'. They have also been selling local businesses an official AD 2000 logo, personally approved by the Pope, in return for 10 per cent of revenue on sales.

The Vatican even has its own supermarket within its walls, for the favoured few, which doesn't advertise, pays no taxes and undercuts all its rivals in Rome. It also has its own Post Office which pretty much guarantees all its deliveries abroad even if only because all Vatican mail is taken to Switzerland and sent on from there.

All this hardly adds up to a good role model in a country where most everything is breaking or broken and local mail hardly ever gets to where it's supposed to. Most public clocks don't run on time. Bells strike in eccentric patterns and all the Romans seem to do with any real efficiency is take a siesta. Also hands are forever reaching out and taking what's not theirs. A travel guide once told me to watch my possessions carefully and, within five minutes of her warning, someone had pinched *her* briefcase. They got my new pyjamas on that trip too. They also, as befits a race where tax evasion is practically a national pastime, hate credit cards. Here cash is always king.

But for a pilgrim to Rome the streets and piazzas are never short of interest or surprise, as when you chance across a massive stone head with staring eyes, just sitting there and looking mighty fed up, having clearly mislaid its body. Or, just nearby, there was this big – and I mean the *biggest* – severed stone hand with its forefinger poking up into the air in a vaguely obscene way. With a thousand Roman fountains too it's a rare piazza that doesn't have some sort of fountain gurgling or dribbling inside it.

The mighty Tiber, as it curled around those seven hills and

massive stone steps, was also a constant source of attentive wonder, flowing peacefully on her way beneath marvellous stone bridges – one bridge was practically airborne with the wings of many stone angels. I also wandered around the old Forum, where the crowds once gathered for chariot races and sea battles, occasionally stopping to shade my eyes as puzzles of sunlight gathered over those massive triumphal arches or all those carefully composed ruins. There are so many ruins in the ancient parts of Rome you might even be picking your way over some rather grand bomb-site and, as yet another broken arch looms over you, fragmented against a blue sky, you often wonder what it must all have been like and how extraordinarily beautiful everything around here must have been when it was all first put up.

And everything was so *big* in this knickerbocker glory of cities. The memorials, the triumphal arches, the broken-backed aqueducts . . . you walk up to them and offer your puny witness to them and, in so doing, often feel, well, so *small*, so totally irrelevant to the mighty sweep of Roman history. Back in Britain we have almost nothing we could put up to almost any of these.

Much of Rome was originally built to inspire faith, and Pope Nicholas V had ordered, way back in 1455, that the city should become as majestic as the Christian faith itself. 'If the authority of the Holy See were visibly displayed in majestic buildings, imperishable memorials and witnesses seemingly planted by the hand of God himself, belief would grow and strengthen like a tradition from one generation to another and all the world would revere it.'

Well, something has clearly gone wrong with his early vision and it was odd to think that I had begun this book in Berlin, where they are busy building everything up, and ending it here in Rome where everything was busy falling down. Even their holy men seemed to have similar dispositions, I was to learn in the course of my research – the fiery, rebellious Luther prepared to take on the Pope and the gentle, poetic Francis who wouldn't hurt a fly.

The peoples themselves couldn't be any more different either: the relentless, energetic Germans and the ditsy, laid-back Italians who were once so bad at war the Germans had to physically encircle them in a ring of steel so that they wouldn't run home to their mothers.

Perhaps holy men do create their own people, and God's active penetration of his world is far deeper and more subtle than we have ever imagined. For those two men had been deeply touched by God – of that I was certain. Ages of darkness followed by ages of light seem to be a historical pattern and the only way we achieve an age of light, history tells us, is through men like Francis and Luther. Men like Christ. Men like us.

—

Listen. 'You can still hear the clash of the gladiators' swords, the roars of the lions and the screams of the victims . . .' A guide was leading a group around the Colosseum, a world-class lump of gorgonzola if ever there was one, full of gaping holes and smashed walls, all connected by bits of modern fencing and wooden walkways put there so visitors can walk around the place. Sunlight lit up some of the corridors in unusual ways while leaving others in the dark. But the very heart of the arena – a ragged collection of exposed corridors, elevators and animal pens – roared with sun. You wanted to feed it all into a computer, give it all a virtual reality and bring it all back to life.

Another group came along, the guide working from the same hymn sheet. 'You can still hear the clash of the gladiators' swords, the roars of the lions and the screams of the victims . . .'

Outside, several scamps were dressed up as Roman centurions complete with plastic helmets and PVC swords, happy to stand with the tourists, preferably young girls, and be photographed for a fee. The snag was they kept grabbing the young girls' tender bits and the girls kept running away from them, some practically sobbing with outrage which got even worse – when the centurions then ran after them and demanded to be paid.

Another unsavoury group who prey on pilgrims to Rome are the gypsy children who actually come walking down the pavement toting large bits of cardboard which they use to disguise the movements of their speedy hands as they lift a purse or camera. Everyone is afraid of these kids – or at least is told to be afraid of them – and the mere sight of one of them wandering towards you fiddling with his bit of cardboard is usually enough to make whole gangs of pilgrims turn on their heels and leg it fast. Pilgrims are warned never, on any account, to touch or interfere with them.

I followed three of these gypsy kids at a discreet distance one afternoon as they skittered through the crowds with their hands darting this way and that. The parents were nowhere to be seen and I imagined them sitting in some sort of Fagin's lair in the Catacombs waiting to receive, with some impatience, whatever their kids had stolen that day.

Certainly the police didn't like getting mixed up with them either and will only 'lift' one under severe provocation since they may well be small but they have large teeth which they will sink into any unwary arm faster than a rattler. I did once see a policeman throw one into the back of a car except the driver, another policeman, who had been sitting there having a quiet smoke, immediately got out of the car, dropped his fag, opened the door, grabbed the kid and flung him out again. Then, as the two policemen argued heatedly, the kid made off so fast you couldn't see him for dust.

Another guide came by with his group saying that, at the height of its activity, the Colosseum seated 45,000 who came in through 80 entrances and sat in four tiers: the first for the great and the good, the second for the middle classes, the third for slaves and foreigners and the fourth for the women and the poor. The groups always laugh at that bit about the women and the poor, he said later. That one always seemed to get them going.

The audience watched fights between midgets with wooden clubs as a warm-up act. Then there were battles between gladiators or men slaughtering wild animals like lions, bears or even giraffes – sometimes as many as 5,000 a day. Thousands of Christians were also famously fed to the lions here. Every effort was made to destroy this subversive sect which disregarded the divine supremacy of the Emperor.

Here then we probably see one of the world's first crucibles of violence and murder as a public entertainment. It was all up and running even then. We come as visitors to Rome and pretend astonishment that they were so vile and decadent in enjoying such sickening spectacles but this primary evil has evolved relentlessly right up to the present day as anyone can see all too clearly when he turns on the television or visits a cinema. The great modern evil of the persistent pursuit of violence for entertainment may even have started in this broken-toothed place with all the awesome consequences for a world now slipping and struggling in a long season of black rain.

Yet we might pause for a while outside the Church of the Santa Maria Sopra Minerva and look at the neighbouring building which once used to be the headquarters of the Inquisition. We might pause and think of a deeply ill man who was being asked exactly what it was he was saying when he wrote his *Dialogues*.

He was humbled and broken, trembling and on his knees. They were threatening this heretic with excommunication, torture, imprisonment and even death. They would certainly find a deeply evil intent in his thinking. Best to plead guilty to all charges, he had been told. Confess all and throw yourself at the mercy of the Holy Office. Put an end to it once and for all. Apologize like you've never apologized before.

> I, Galileo, Florentine, aged 70 years, arraigned personally before this tribunal and kneeling before You, Most Reverend and Eminent Lord Cardinals, Inquisitors-General against heretical depravity throughout the Christian commonwealth, having before my eyes and touching with my hands the Holy Gospels, swear that I have always believed, believe now, and with God's help I will in future believe all that is held, preached and taught by the Holy Catholic and Apostolic Church. But whereas – after being admonished by this Holy Office entirely to abandon the false opinion that the Sun is the centre of the world and immovable, and that the Earth is not the centre of the same and that it moves, and that I must not hold, defend nor teach in any manner whatever, either orally or in writing, the said false doctrine, and after it had been notified to me that the said doctrine was contrary to Holy Writ – I wrote and caused to be printed a book in which I treat of the already condemned doctrine, and adduce arguments of much efficacy in its favour, without arriving at any solution: I have been judged vehemently suspected of heresy, that is, of having held and believed that the Sun is the centre of the world and immovable, and that the earth is not the centre and moves.
>
> Therefore, wishing to remove from the minds of your Eminences and of all faithful Christians this vehement suspicion justly conceived against me, I abjure with a sincere heart and unfeigned faith, I curse and detest the said errors and heresies, and generally all and every error and sect contrary to the Holy Catholic Church. And I swear that for the future I will never again say nor assert in speaking or writing

> such things as may bring upon me similar suspicion: and if I know of any heretic, or person suspected of heresy, I will denounce him to the Holy Office, or to the Inquisitor. I also swear and promise to adopt and observe entirely all the penances which may have to be imposed on me by this Holy Office. And if I contravene any of these said promises, protests or oaths (which God forbid!), I submit myself to all the pains and penalties imposed and promulgated by all the Sacred Canons and other Decrees, general and particular, against such offenders. So help me God and these His Holy Gospels which I touch with my own hands.
>
> I, the said Galileo Galilei, have abjured, sworn, promised and bound myself as above; and in witness of the truth, with my own hand have subscribed the present document of my abjuration and have recited it word by word in Rome, at the Convent of the Minerva, this 22nd day of June 1633.

But still the earth moves, some say he then said under his breath. *Still the earth moves*. Many more have said that he was so frightened it wouldn't have been possible. Yet even after this gold-medal winning apology punishment was withering and swift.

> We condemn you to the formal prison of this Holy Office during our pleasure, and by way of salutary penance we enjoin that for three years to come you repeat once a week the seven Penitential Psalms. Reserving to ourselves liberty to moderate, commute, or take off, in whole or in part, the aforesaid penalties and penance.

His book was also to be banned and has remained on the Index of Prohibited Books for 200 years. And so it was that Copernican thinking was given a decent burial. The heretic Galileo was broken on the wheel and the Supreme Pontiff was proved right yet again. Not.

The earth still moves.

But it was soon clear that this severe punishment was largely framed to put the wind up Galileo, who was soon returned to his home in Florence and the love of his eldest daughter Maria Celeste. He was to write one more book, *Discourses*, a brilliant account of the way mathematics describes the real world. But he later went blind and died in 1642 even though the spirit of Galileo still lives, still impelling us to explore and understand the universe in which we find ourselves still mysteriously revolving.

I continued wandering the streets of Rome for several days in that golden autumn looking for the end of my pilgrimage and this book. I didn't know what form it might take, only that it had to be somewhere in these streets. But where? Nothing obvious was presenting itself, although my wanderings kept throwing up lots of odd and even bizarre moments. Anyone with a clear eye and a few years to spare should get to know these streets since there must be a great Latin *Ulysses* just hanging around on these dusty corners and waiting to be written.

Early one night I got on a tram near the Piazza Maggiore which began clattering along for about a hundred yards when it stopped and refused to go again. A lot of the passengers began grumbling volubly, throwing their hands up into the air in disgust or poking their forefingers into their mouths as if about to be sick. I looked around at this lot carefully and realized that, apart from a few old women in black, almost all of them were as drunk as monkeys.

The driver began rummaging around under his seat and took out one of the biggest sledgehammers I have ever seen. He then climbed down into the street and laid about this tram with his sledgehammer like an enraged Latin Basil Fawlty. *Bang, crash, wallop*. Everyone in the tram, even the old women in black, seemed to be cheering wildly as he continued his demented attack on this poor tram. *Bang, crash, wallop*. The very blows shook our fillings loose and the passengers' joy was unconfined when the engine exploded into life. The driver put away his sledgehammer under the seat, climbed back into the tram, bowed to the cheering mob and, in a trice, the tram got on its clattering way.

I wasn't too sure what I would find in the Vatican Museum, although I did pick up an extremely bad mood in there since the authorities have devised a route of the most intricate torture ensuring that you go into every room and see every last Etruscan coin and bed-pan until, exhausted, you finally get to the Sistine Chapel where you can stand, but not sit, staring up at the great ceiling through a rising tide of body odour and bored children's squalls.

But even in such a bad mood and on such a hot, sweaty day, I could see that these were frescoes like no other, full of life and space and movement. You could almost still see Michelangelo up there, shouting at the Pope and complaining about paint in his beard, as he put together this vast and effortless homage to God in which the many people are like gods and the gods are like people. The ceiling has portraits of the drunkenness of Noah and works its way back to the Creation of Light above the altar. This vast and accomplished work may even be the first great celebration of artistic creativity. Michelangelo, the supreme orderer of space and time, was always seeking to catch the supreme moment, and here we have a moment when all art is pure and first realizing its ordained role of offering us the clean and replenishing rain of heaven. And the greatest of these moments was right there with a powerful and bearded God leaning across the hands and arms of a group of angels and stretching out to Adam, creating crackles of energy between their outstretched fingers: the very energy that keeps us all going – the mystery and wonder of life itself.

We have in it all a fantastically exuberant celebration of the human body, I think, although it was not to everyone's taste and Pope Hadrian VI dismissed it as a 'bathroom of nudes'. But he couldn't have got it more wrong. The very spirit of God is in those murals and Michelangelo's work was one of the primary engines of the Italian Renaissance, soon to be attacked by the perversions, grotesqueries and cruelties of an increasingly secular age. Quiet understatement gave way to lurid exaggeration. The normal became the perverted. Delicacy and irony gave way to violence and harshness. Artistic minds began teeming with monsters which they were not slow to unleash on a sleeping world.

In spite of the crowds, beggary and heat I did manage to wallow in a certain spiritual grandeur the next day in the rather unlikely setting of St Peter's Church itself. It was a lonely, if comforting day as, with guide book in hand, I worked my way around almost every part of it, feeding on such as the fluent grace of Michelangelo's *Pietà* or rubbing my hand over the foot of a bronze statue of St Peter.

But the main feature of this church is that, as befits the principal shrine of the Catholic Church, it is so colossal that mere crowds never seem to impinge on its space. There *were* crowds in there but, as I wandered around, I almost had the feeling of being alone, of being the last pilgrim in the world just walking around this huge place hand in hand with God.

So how do you manage to keep this place warm in winter then? Are there any times when people really get on your nerves? What's the most unusual prayer you have ever heard? Did you actually answer it, did you?

This strange feeling of aloneness gripped me so completely I again kept thinking of Jerusalem and another pilgrimage I had made there on the eve of the Gulf War. All the restaurants were closed and everyone seemed to have disappeared after

Saddam Hussein had promised to destroy the country in a sea of fire. The Via Dolorosa was deserted as was the Church of the Holy Sepulchre. The only people in Manger Square in Bethlehem were soldiers on the rooftops watching my every move with their binoculars.

It was the one time in my life when I felt close to and almost completely at one with God. We actually revelled in one another's company and here now, in St Peter's, was another pilgrim moment of loving closeness.

Even high up in the roof where I was alone, standing on a ledge and hearing almost nothing at all, I felt I was all but inside the breathing lungs of God. They moved in and out steadily, warmly, *humanly*. I paused, half expecting he might have something to say. But he never does when you expect it.

I looked directly down onto the huge canopy said to be built directly over the spot where St Peter had been buried. It would be nice, I suppose, to add St Peter's coffin to my collection of holy touches and it might even have given me an end to this book if I could have worked out some way of doing it. But I couldn't physically get at it. And there is some doubt that Peter is actually down there. Yet they did excavate the tomb recently and found the skeleton of a man who may have been his size.

But here on the roof, looking out over the Eternal City and feeling warmly enclosed in the lungs of God, I found myself thinking back over my autumn pilgrimage. And even as I thought of The Road, with all its twists and turns, my mind also began putting together a prayer of praise and thanks for what had been such a wonderful journey.

That half-bombed church in Berlin reared up briefly followed by that miraculous resurrection morning when I had woken up in a dew-drenched meadow in Wittenberg. The tinkling sounds of that harpsichord playing Bach in the garden of his home in Erfurt came to me as did the sight of that dog playing in the fountain in Leipzig. Then there was the larky humour of that chapel in Colditz and the sweet way that river wound its way around that meadow in Oberammergau. I don't suppose I will ever forget my first sight of the Grand Canal in Venice or that bat-fluttered sunset in Verona or that golden Sunday morning in Florence.

But other odd things kept surfacing in my memory too. Those deer standing by the speeding autobahn and that scruffy Oxfam hassock of St Francis which still got me laughing whenever I recalled it. My hands can also still feel the touch of metal of St Mark's coffin: a marvellous highlight to any pilgrimage if ever there was one.

Yet there was another level to it all too in the shape of dreams of dancing coelacanths and the holy man floating just beneath the clear water of a stream. Hallucinations in squares. Hammering hands and laughter in mists. Visits from famous men, conjured out of the special joy of those times as I searched for them in their own landscapes, reaching out to them and trying to make them a part of my personal experience, wondering how I could make their strengths my strengths.

We all make our pilgrimages in our own ways; journeys like these take us into life itself and onto the very doorstep of God. We *find* God on The Road, not only in the majestic paintings of the Uffizi but in the demented driver beating his tram with a sledgehammer; not just in a towering basilica in Assisi but in the sighs of that woman so carefully and lovingly studying the photographs of her children on the Rome subway.

In all these diverse images and actions we keep finding the attributes and qualities of God and we then also begin to start understanding his divine purpose which is only ever to be like himself. Certainly I could never remember a time when I had ever been so close to him. Oh sure, there had been fallings out as on my visit to Dachau but my pleasure became his pleasure and my unfolding prayer in St Peter's became a special prayer of thanks that we had found such a special time with one another out on The Road. You always touch God when you touch life, which is where he actually lives.

And it seemed right too that this long, unfolding pilgrim prayer came bubbling up in this fine church in which this complex God of ours can work and relax; a real home in which he can enjoy the music of worship or the words of prayer; a place of echoing emptiness where he can wander as the mood takes him. *So this is where you hang out, is it? But tell me one thing now. Would you call this your main residence or is it just a summer home? And another thing. What's the stupidest prayer you've ever heard? Do you ever actually clamp your hands over your ears?*

But even as my journey made its way along the path of this prayer and into yet another conversation with him, I couldn't quite see it as the end of this book. I wanted something else to bring it to a proper end, whatever a proper end might be, and I had even begun asking God about this too, telling him that, after such a memorable journey, on which I'd had more than a fair share of pilgrim luck, I didn't want it all to just fade away or simply fizzle out in the disappointing way that life often does. I wanted the final scene to stand up proudly and defiantly.

Yet nothing was coming and I was beginning to get anxious about going home particularly as my advance had all but run out. I just couldn't hang around any longer. Then, later that day, I was sitting on the doorstep of my camper eating a Pot Noodle with a fork – it wasn't *much* of an advance – when I actually *heard* the end I had been looking for. It was an explosion so loud and unexpected it made me drop my fork. I thought it might even have been a terrorist bomb, since those idiots have long been active in Italy, when I picked up on a sudden chill in the air and spotted a huge, black cloud, thick with rain, rolling in over the outlying hills.

Even as the thunder rumbled angrily again and the first

raindrops fell, my face lit up with a smile larger than the Pope's. 'Yes,' I shouted, dropping my Pot Noodle. 'Yes, yes, yes.' It was the perfect finale really, so I hopped into my camper and drove straight back into the heart of the Eternal City since my days in warm fields of gold had really come to an end with a massive storm about to break out over Rome.

It pretty much came pumping down when it started, whole torrents of it, bringing the traffic largely to a standstill and forcing a lot of the moped riders to take shelter under the bridges where they had a smoke or stood around chatting to one another. Men were walking along the pavements with plastic carrier bags on their heads as giant puddles began swelling up out of the gutters, already blocked by the falling leaves, and spilling out over the roads. You never quite knew how deep those puddles were either, and I had to call up a certain level of faith as I drove into them where even my heavy camper seemed to be aqua-planing as I carried on into the next one. A big, bright flower stall with no customers swirled into view.

Another roll of milky thunder, another crack of lightning and whole buckets of rain were now pouring on everyone and everything, raining on Catholic and Protestant, raining on cardinal and beggar, raining on the ruins of the ancient city and the barricades and balconies of the Spanish Steps, raining on the vast edifice of the Vittorio Emanuelle monument, built to commemorate unification and also containing the Tomb of the Unknown Soldier, raining on the huge Piazza Venezia and raining on the balcony where Mussolini made his rousing speeches about how he was going to get all the trains to run on time.

Everyone and everything was soaked in equal measure in this wonderfully democratic downpour and you kept noticing the odd tricks that rain can do with light; the way that the uneven torrents can, for example, actually compress the street lights against the roofs like flattened halos before letting them expand again when the torrents slowed.

Lightning flashed over the Tiber, briefly illuminating the ornate stone bridges and moored houseboats. There are six million trees in Rome and everywhere leaves rode the tumbling river like brown, racing coracles as lightning cracked again. It might have been the setting for yet another Sack of Rome as when the angry Lutherans poured down into the city from the North in 1527, killing half the population. A young man ran down the pavement with his head held low and shoulders hunched. A businessman was frantically trying to wave down a taxi with his briefcase.

Near the Trevi I got out of my camper to walk down the narrow, thundering streets to the fountain. The rain caused so much diffusion you were never quite sure if the lights were on or off. Light kept mysteriously breaking down into darkness before being pushed back again. Occasionally the very skies seemed to be strangely affected when an iridescent crown of bright gold briefly took up position above the towers and rooftops before slipping back into dripping darkness again. Where do pigeons go in the rain? What do pigeons do to pass away the time when it's too wet to go out?

The lights inside the cafés were constant enough with groups huddled together over the tables, mostly communing with bottles of wine while others were playing backgammon. Tourists never seem to know what to do in the rain. It never features in holiday brochures so they don't know what to do when it starts. Rain foxes them completely. Many go to bed or drink too much. *Forget the Trevi and have a Bevy*, one charming restaurant sign suggested.

But who could ever forget the Trevi? This fountain is so popular they fish out over £2,000 a week in foreign coins, I heard a guide tell his group and, even in this relentless downpour, there was still quite a crowd on the steps in front of it, all gazing up at this marvellous, illuminated spillage of water over a huge tangle of statues all springing fully-formed out of the rough rocks.

The Italians excel at such fountains; creating these exuberant rushing cataracts of water, full of dancing light and waltzing movement. Such imaginative sculptures of light and sound can be seen as constantly moving paintings; they erupt with possibly God's greatest and most primary gift of water while a whole religion was once based on these silvery miracles to the extent that a decree had to be issued which forbade the worship of fountains.

This corner has also become another shrine to romantic love and there are many who still try to wade into the water following the example of Anita Ekberg in *La Dolce Vita*. Unless the police manage to grab them first. Lightning flashed and another roll of thunder came ripping down through the outlying alleyways with all the authority of a declaration of war. A newly married couple turned up to be photographed against the backdrop of the fountain, she still in her bridal gown and trying hard to smile in the rain and him in a dress suit which was so wet he was surely going to have a lot of difficulty explaining it all when he took it back to Moss Bros in the morning. But everyone watched the photographer do his work with a sort of gooey smile. Weddings are wonderful for raising gooey smiles. They remind us of the times when we were young and beautiful and full of hope; the time when everything that was fine was before us just sitting there waiting to be picked up.

More by luck than design my pluvial travels that night finally brought me down to St Peter's Square where I was able to stand under the giant colonnades and look out over this famous square which, for the moment, had been fully and finally rinsed of all pilgrims and pigeons.

Nothing moved in the pouring rain except the odd African

who seemed to materialize out of the very puddles before trying to sell me a bunch of flowers or an umbrella and then disappearing again just as mysteriously. Yet it was a fine moment nonetheless as I stood there looking out at the abandoned canopy which the Pope had sat under for his Wednesday audience and then up at the dark silhouettes of the apostles as they lined up on the church's roof like some medieval stone army poised to go on some new crusade to steal another holy body from the Turks in Constantinople.

Just over there was the roof where white puffs of smoke went up when the cardinals managed to elect a new Pope. Our present Pope was probably lying abed behind one of those windows up there, possibly smiling within one of his holy dreams or else just stretched out there and looking up at the rain just like the rest of us. It was oddly comforting to realize that even Popes have to sleep, even if Pope Urban, the one who had hounded Galileo, was such a notorious light sleeper he ordered all the song birds killed in the Vatican gardens because they kept waking him up.

A low-flying plane with flickering lights droned through the murky skies like an angel in a hurry to get home to its partner and a warm bed. I wanted to get home to my own warm, dry bed in Wales too and was quite happy with this as the final scene for my book, particularly as the Reformation had been started in Germany largely because of Luther's objection to the sale of Indulgences to actually finance the building of this great church here in Italy.

As I stood there in the rain it seemed a sort of historical metaphor which tied my pilgrimage up into an unusually neat bundle. Pilgrimages never come in unusually neat bundles any more than books do. Pilgrimages are often messy and unpredictable – like life itself.

But to be perfectly honest, almost *anything* would have looked good to me and my corpse-strewn notebook as I stood under that colonnade soaking wet and already sneezing ominously. Even a poke in the eye by a policeman would have seemed a good ending to this book at that moment and all I was really worried about was whether I'd got enough in my memory and notebook to actually write a full-length book when I got home. But writers always worry about such things when the truth is they usually have an almost mystical intuition when they've got enough. Just.

Yet, almost more than anything else, I was pleased that I had repaired my relationship with God on The Road and, just looking around me at a holy, rainswept square, where so many millions of pilgrims before me must also have revived and sustained their love affair with God, I could actually *feel* him smiling warmly. He was smiling with the promise that there will always be renewal after exhaustion; that even in our darkest seasons of black rain he will always send down this, the clean rain of heaven which will also, in time, bring forth new life from the charred and smoking fields of a dead harvest.

Yes, the earth moves and will always keep moving as long as I'm in charge.

And so my pilgrimage through the many and varied dreams of God to the Eternal City came to an end. My long drive into an endless autumnal wonder was over. Not with another startling vision or a strange hallucination. But to the sound of a bell in a night of Roman rain. With the Pope smiling in his sleep nearby. With another sneeze under a colonnade. With another flashing revelation of lightning and another roll of thunder. And with yet another forceful African materializing out of a puddle and trying to sell me an umbrella.